1000 Little Chats with God
And you can listen too!

Bryan White

First Printing: 16 May 2016

ISBN-13: 978-1533273758

Foreword

You do not cross paths with individuals like Bryan White on accident. From observing his interactions with others and the manner in which they perceive him. You were intended to meet him. He has a way of making an impression upon you from himself without altering you or your perception of others. I met him when I pledged Omega Psi Phi Fraternity and he was in the position to review all applications. I had spoken to several others that were already Omega Men and they gave me his contact information.

Being much older than Bryan and what I felt, much more experienced in life, I did not expect to be impressed. I have had several life experiences myself and it was rare that my encounters with others ever impressed or interested me after five minutes of the initial contact but Bryan was quite different.

Although at first it was only through text messages there was the way he approached me. He or his fraternity did not require my entrance into the fraternity to sustain their organization yet his contact with me was humble and unassuming. I was already very interested in the organization but I wanted to know more about this guy, what's his story.

As a Financial Planner, he asked me to meet him at his school so we could discuss his financial future and that is where I saw him at his best. Bryan is a guidance councilor at a colorfully diverse middle school in Nashville Tennessee. I often had the privilege to watch him interact with his students. His matter of fact approach to real issues that affect them has allowed him to communicate on a level to them that could not be duplicated by another educator. In one of my visits I stopped at a gas station nearby and a woman approached me from behind and said "Bryan White is that you'. When I turned around she said "oh I thought you were Bryan White" I laughed and said, "No but I know him, what did he do now?" "Nothing but turn my son's life around." 'He was headed the wrong direction early but he got on Bryan's wrestling team and everything changed". If you are around Bryan or you know him, you will here stories like this often.

As I compiled the prayers for this book we originally planned to list them chronologically and by relevancy but I have noticed as I read them myself, that they are timeless and always relevant to a situation. The prayers from his post come from different times in his life, and different times in our social consciousness yet they always work. No matter where you open this book and began reading it will feel good and pleasant.

I am of the Islamic faith but after I read a few of his "conversations" with God I was impressed. Others I have listened to or read seemed to be talking to God but "showing out" for the audience or to receive some type of praise or accolades from their peers when the ultimate goal of a prayer is to ask God for guidance and protection.

Normally the "About the Author" section is saved for a few lines of the jacket of a book but in Bryan's case we think you should read about his life in its entirety because it helps explain the depth of his life. This depth has allowed him to have wonderful conversations with God that he does not mind sharing with others. Bryan is my Friend, a mentor and a brother and I am proud to be a part of his project. We hope, to you this is a book that you never stop reading.

Very infrequently does one happen upon something that changes him/her to the very core. Something so simple, yet so profound, that expecting life to remain the same after having encountered it is the ultimate task in futility.

I am a lover of words; always have been. When my best friend, Kelvin McClendon, suggested that I read a few of the pennings of a good friend of his, I agreed. The sincerity and humble nature of Mr. White's words are beyond moving, they, as I have stated earlier, stir one to the very soul. I was no exception.

It is my prayer that those who find themselves between the covers of this book also find the strength, motivation, and hope that they seek.

Well done, Mr. White. Well done.

Dr. Chance McLin

INTRODUCTION

I was born in Brooklyn, New York on March 3, 1972 to a registered nurse and a UPS driver (former Marine). I was raised in a single parent home with no siblings. I spent a lot of time alone as my mother often worked long hours at multiple jobs. She worked so much; I remember hating her for always working and not spending time with me. I only saw my father on weekends and then I had to share that time as he was commissioner of a softball league so we travelled from park to park on Sunday watching games (although I played softball when I got older, to this day, I hate baseball/softball). My extended family of cousins, aunts and uncles were great, we spent many weekends just being together and creating memories.

My mom being the youngest of her siblings and always one to create her own path in life decided that we would move to South Carolina when I was 11 or 12, she said it was to give me a better life. I hated every minute of it, I learned to love it, as there was no way out but I wasn't going to stay in Brooklyn with my father. After moving to SC, what little relationship I had with my father became extinct. I would be another 12 to 15 years before we were able to salvage our relationship and when it got really good, he passed away.

Mom became a foster parent when I was in high school. This brought her lots of joy! I on the other hand was not so much impressed. I decided upon a major in college (Psychology) based on one foster child that had come into the home. I entered the University of South Carolina in 1989. At first, college was very hard for me, why, I really don't know. My program director, a black male told me that I was never going to make it and that I should go home. I was determined to prove him wrong. Once I found my lane, school was rewarding. I graduated with 2 degrees (Psychology and African-American Studies). I attended Graduate School at the University of Mississippi, I again met difficulty. I was told once again, by a black male (Dean of the College) I was not smart enough to be there and that I needed to go home and stop wasting my parent's money. The struggle was real! I knew I had to see it through when the one person I had never seen quit or utter the words "I can't" said "it's ok if you don't finish." With prayer and lots of hard work, I earned 2 Masters Degrees and 30 hours toward a 3rd as well as going on to represent the University at a national conference.

I moved to Nashville in August of 2000, I was employed by an SEC school as an Academic Advisor for Student-Athletes. That tenure did not last very long, lots of changes and difference in view point lead to me having to seek other employment. This time proved very trying for me. I had just gotten married, just bought a new home and we were expecting our first child. Prayer and attending church had always been a part of my life. Prior to marriage, I had actually begun to seek a closer relationship with God.

The job loss in 2003 really strengthened that relationship. I began to read the bible more, in turn it made the weekly sermons that much more interesting as I felt connected and had an understanding of what was going on. I did not mention earlier that ALL of my schooling in Brooklyn was a private Christian Schools; I had been equipped with a "rough draft" of sorts very early in life. My prayer life evolved out of desperation! I asked for at least 6 months to get myself back together, and God kept his word, for 6 months we never missed a mortgage payment, services were never cut off, food was always in the house and gas was in the cars. I learned that prayer works.

I mentioned Mom became a foster parent; she had at least half a dozen or so children over a 10 year period. 3 boys stuck with her through it all, although she formally only adopted 1. When Mom moved to Nashville, 2 of the 3 boys eventually did too. One, in particular was having some life difficulties, I began praying for him via a text message group I created. The group evolved as social media grew. I began to post prayers to my Facebook page morning and evening. It wasn't long before others began to comment how the prayers really spoke to them and their situation. I never really thought about it, as they were really only for one person. Friends and Family began to look for these prayers daily, I felt like this was something I was supposed to do, not for gain of any sort, just because it was the right thing to do. At a low time I was speaking with my mother telling her that I was cutting back on posting these prayers, for no other reason than the one they were directed to at the time was having the hardest time. She told me that I needed to continue and that the impact was greater than I was aware. She reminded me that I was causing trouble in the atmosphere. I was encouraging people to pray daily. She cautioned me like she always does and said "when you do this, there will be things that happen that will try to knock you off course, get ready and stay focused", she told me that I could not let the enemy win. I didn't really understand her words until I got that phone call from the police asking that I come in for questioning, I had been accused of physically abusing my youngest son. This episode was really hard on my family, lots of questions, interviews and evaluations, and I, through it all, I kept praying and believing and then another phone call comes in a few months later "all charges have been dropped"! I am not where I want to be, but I am happy where I am. I continue to post a prayer at least 5 days a week. I have been blessed above and beyond where I saw my life going. I am the father of 4 children and the husband of 1 wife. I am employed by the local school system as a Professional School Counselor as well as being a small business owner.

I rise this morning to kneel before your throne of greatness. I pray for continued grace and mercy and forgiveness of my sins. I thank You for finding favor in this cracked vessel. Fill me up with your spirit and use me to help another. In Jesus Name! Amen.

Father God, thank You for waking us and for being so merciful by giving us another chance to Behold Your Glory. You continue to give us all that we need and do much more than we deserve. Thank you for Grace, Mercy and Your Peace. In Jesus Name! Amen

Thank You for allowing my eyes to open and my lungs to inflate. I pray for the families of those who did not make it to this point today. My prayers are specifically directed this day toward those who are dealing with depression during this season. Use your children to be that light that someone may need to see. Father I pray that I am walking and working in your Will. In good times and bad times help me to continue to walk by Faith. In Jesus Name! Amen.

Thank You Lord for the unconditional Love that you have shown me. Your grace has blessed me with yet another undeserved day. I pray for my fellow man and I do for myself. Bless me so that I may help to bless another. Remove those things from me that are not pleasing in your sight. Keep my mind focused on You. In Jesus Name! Amen.

Thank You for this new day filled with blessings. I praise your name for you have allowed me to see a new day, not promised to any, not granted to all. Allow me compassion for my fellow man and the will to go above and beyond when difficult times arise. Give to me Lord so I may give to another. In Jesus Name! Amen.

Thank You, Lord for hearing the prayers of a sinner and allowing me to see another day. I Thank You for this day because it becomes more clear everyday that another day is not promised. I pray for the families and the loved ones who have once again been involved in an act of selfish and senseless violence. Protect us from ourselves Dear Lord. Encourage us to treat others as we desire to be treated. In Jesus Name! Amen.

Heavenly Father, I rise this morning giving extreme Thanks for blessing me with another day. Teach me to use those talents that you have developed within me to go beyond myself and to uplift another. Send your peace our way, because, we as a people need you more than ever in times such as these. In Jesus Name! Amen.

I thank You for waking me this morning! I pray that you will continue to teach me to lean on you regardless of the height of the mountain or the depth of the valley, or even how dim the outcome may seem, with these human eyes. Strengthen my Faith Lord! Remind me that as long as I keep my eyes on the Son, I will not drown. In Jesus Name! Amen.

Heavenly Father I Thank You for last night's slumber. I am even more grateful that you have allowed me to wake to this new day. I pray that you would forgive me of my sins and indiscretions. Allow me to grow closer to you and to always seek your face. I pray that you would send peace in the midst of the constant turmoil surrounding so many of us. Bless me so that I may bless another
In Jesus Name! Amen.

I rise this morning giving Thanks! Thank You for allowing me to see another day, Thank You for my health, mentally, physically and spiritually. Thank You for my family and loved ones. Let me not look at what others have and negate the blessings you have sent my way. Allow me to live a more humble, less self centered life. In Jesus Name! Amen.

Heavenly Father, I thank You for opening my eyes and filling my lungs with air this morning. On this day that we gather to give Thanks, let us remember those who may not be as fortunate as we currently are. Let our hearts be void of selfishness. Remind us that it is during this season that many will be plagued with depression and isolation. We aim to uplift one another this day and every day. In Jesus Name! Amen.

Heavenly Father I thank You for last night's slumber. I am even more grateful that you have allowed me to wake to this new day. I pray that you would forgive me of my sins and indiscretions. Allow me to grow closer to you and to always seek your face. I pray that you would send peace in the midst of the constant turmoil surrounding so many of us. Bless me so that I may bless another
In Jesus Name! Amen.

Thank You, Lord for the blessing of another day. I pray that I use the gifts and talents you have so graciously given me to help another. Let prideful behavior and self conceit flee far from me. I pray that you flood the lives of your children with blessings that man cannot comprehend. In Jesus Name! Amen.

I lift my voice this morning praising your name for allowing me to wake in my right mind with full control of my limbs. I praise you because you are worthy. I thank You for the many blessings that have come my way. Father, please keep my family, friends and loved ones safe. Remove selfish tendencies and keep me humble. In Jesus Name! Amen.

Thank You, Lord for opening my eyes to this new day that you have so perfectly designed. I pray that I might, this day live up to the expectations and potential that you have placed on and within me. Keep me humble yet teachable at all times. Make me fast to think and slow to speak. In Jesus Name! Amen.

Heavenly Father, I rise this morning extremely grateful that you have seen fit to allow me to see another day. I pray that my actions and words represent your hand on my life. In Jesus Name! Amen.

Most Gracious and Loving Heavenly Father I Thank You for last night's slumber and this morning's wake up call. I ask that You would continue to bring out the best in me even when I don't recognize my own potential for greatness. I pray for peace at home and at work. Send healing to the sick and provide the downtrodden with uplift. In Jesus Name! Amen.

Thank You, Lord for the new day. I pray for those dealing with loss and separation due to location, situation or circumstance. Draw us to you Lord in good times, bad times and all times in between. Remind us to acknowledge you and not our own faulty understanding and interpretations. Keep up surrounded by your hedge of protection so that we may be safe from harm, hurt or danger. In Jesus Name! Amen.
hank You Lord for blessing me with a new day. Thank You for keeping this imperfect vessel safe from harm hurt or danger. I send up prayers of health, healing and restoration this day. In Jesus Name! Amen.

Thank You for this new day and the opportunities therein. Lord I ask that you not let us not be so full of pride that we reject the calling to serve our fellow man. Teach us to flee from selfish thought and action. Keep us humble yet teachable as we deal with others who may not subscribe to this same set of rules. Bless us above and beyond so we can bless another abundantly.

I rise this morning thanking You for the grace and mercy that you have shown me. I am ever grateful for another chance to receive a blessing as well as be a blessing.
Lord, I ask that you cover all who read this prayer. Allow not one of us to miss the blessings that our headed our way, neither allow us to be drawn away from you. Let our light so shine individually and collectively. In Jesus Name! Amen.

Thank You, Lord for allowing me to wake and see a new day. I pray for the families of those whose name was not called on this morning's roll. I pray for forgiveness of sins that serve to separate us from you. Keep us ever mindful that we should pray for one another and strive to treat others as we want to be treated. In Jesus Name! Amen

Thank You, Lord for allowing me to see another day. I Thank You for the protection afforded me while I slumbered. Father, please strengthen me so that the storms of life don't alter my

perspective, but instead increase my praise. For I know if I keep my eyes on the son I will be saved.
In Jesus Name! Amen.

Thank You, Lord for allowing me to see another day. I Thank You for the protection afforded me while I slumbered. Father, please strengthen me so that the storms of life don't alter my perspective, but instead increase my praise. For I know if I keep my eyes on the son I will be saved.
In Jesus Name! Amen.

Thanking You always and in All ways for allowing me to partake in this new day that you have set in motion. Keep my mind focused on you in good times and bad. Remind me that you are the author and finisher of my life, and that all I have is because of you, where I am is where you have brought me and all I know you have taught me. I pray for peace and understanding. In Jesus Name! Amen.

Heavenly Father, thank You for filling my nostrils with your breath. You have so graciously allowed me another opportunity to receive your blessings and to use those blessings to uplift and bless another. I pray that your spirit will be so moved that sickness is healed, depression is erased and that goodness and mercy will follow us all the days of our lives. In Jesus Name! Amen.

Thank You Lord for last night's laying down and this morning's waking up. I thank You for the many blessings great and small that you have allowed into my life. Teach me to walk by faith and not by sight, as what I see if often incomplete and obstructed by the evils of the world. Pour out blessings onto your children. In Jesus Name! Amen.

Heavenly Father I enter into your presence this morning thanking You for blessing me with another day. I Thank You for your grace and mercy that allows me yet another undeserved opportunity to receive your blessings. Surround me and my loved ones with your hedge of protection so that no harm, hurt or danger will come our way. We Love You Lord and we praise your name. In Jesus Name!

Thank You, Lord for blessing me with a new day. Thank You for keeping this imperfect vessel safe from harm hurt or danger. I send up prayers of health, healing and restoration this day. In Jesus Name! Amen.

Thank You for this new day and the opportunities therein. Lord I ask that you not let us no be so full of pride that we reject the calling to serve our fellow man. Teach us to flee from selfish thought and action. Keep us humble yet teachable as we deal with others who may not subscribe to this same set of rules. Bless us above and beyond so we can bless another abundantly.

I rise this morning thanking You for the grace and mercy that you have shown me. I am ever grateful for another chance to receive a blessing as well as be a blessing.

Lord, I ask that you cover all who read this prayer. Allow not one of us to miss the blessings that our headed our way, neither allow us to be drawn away from you. Let our light so shine individually and collectively. In Jesus Name! Amen.

Thank You, Lord for allowing me to wake and see a new day. I pray for the families of those whose name was not called on this morning's roll. I pray for forgiveness of sins that serve to separate us from you. Keep us ever mindful that we should pray for one another and strive to treat others as we want to be treated. In Jesus Name! Amen

Thank You, Lord for allowing me to see another day. I Thank You for the protection afforded me while I slumbered. Father, please strengthen me so that the storms of life don't alter my perspective, but instead increase my praise. For I know if I keep my eyes on the son I will be saved.

In Jesus Name! Amen.

Thank You, Lord for allowing me to see another day. I Thank You for the protection afforded me while I slumbered. Father, please strengthen me so that the storms of life don't alter my perspective, but instead increase my praise. For I know if I keep my eyes on the son I will be saved.

In Jesus Name! Amen.

Thanking You always and in All ways for allowing me to partake in this new day that you have set in motion. Keep my mind focused on you in good times and bad. Remind me that you are the author and finisher of my life, and that all I have is because of you, where I am is where you have brought me and all I know you have taught me. I pray for peace and understanding. In Jesus Name! Amen.

Heavenly Father, thank You for filling my nostrils with your breath. You have so graciously allowed me another opportunity to receive your blessings and to use those blessings to uplift and bless another. I pray that your spirit will be so moved that sickness is healed, depression is erased and that goodness and mercy will follow us all the days of our lives. In Jesus Name! Amen.

Thank You Lord for last night's laying down and this morning's waking up. I thank You for the many blessings great and small that you have allowed into my life. Teach me to walk by faith and not by sight, as what I see if often incomplete and obstructed by the evils of the world. Pour out blessings onto your children. In Jesus Name! Amen.

Heavenly Father I enter into your presence this morning thanking You for blessing me with another day. I Thank You for your grace and mercy that allows me yet another undeserved opportunity to receive your blessings. Surround me and my loved ones with your hedge of protection so that no harm, hurt or danger will come our way. We Love You Lord and we praise your name. In Jesus Name!

Thank You Lord for blessing me with another day. I Thank You for the extension of your grace and mercy toward me. Lord I know you have a plan for my life. I pray for the direction to follow it and the patience to see it through. Remind me to bring my burdens to you and leave them with you, never to pick them up again. In Jesus Name! Amen.

Thank You, Lord for allowing me to open my eyes this morning. I Thank You for a sound mind and a willing body. I pray for forgiveness of sins and the removal of those things from my life that would draw me away from you. Help me to not worry or stress about things I have no control over, instead, teach me how to make YOU my everything. Today I pray for those who need a turnaround in their jobs, finances or relationships. Bless us so we can be a blessing to another. In Jesus Name! Amen.

Thank You Lord for the air that fills my lungs this morning. Lord, as you continue to work on me and in me, I ask that you show me how to not continue to make the same mistakes. I pray that you will forever remind me to always seek your wise council being careful to move in step with your will. Keep those in the midst and path of the SC Flood safe from harm or hurt. In Jesus Name! Amen

Thank You, Lord for again blessing me to see another day. I pray that you would forgive me of my sins of commission and omission. Today and everyday day, I pray for healing for the sick. Give me strength this day to carry on when things get rough, while making room for compassion for my fellow man. Bless my fellow man as you so richly continue to bless me. In Jesus Name! Amen.

Thank You Lord for blessing me with another day. I rise knowing that whatever this day brings, you are still in control. I pray for the families in SC affected by the rising waters. Give them peace in the middle of the storm. I ask for blessings for all. In Jesus Name! Amen.

All praise due to You My Lord, My God. Thank You for keeping me safe while I slept and allowing me to see another day. Father my prayers go out to those in the path of the storm. Keep them safe as the winds blow and the rain falls. Father, allow my words to be used to uplift my fellow man cause me to think twice before I speak. In Jesus Name! Amen.

Thank You, Lord for this new day and the many blessings within. I thank You for your grace and mercy which has kept me safe. I Thank You for health and always pray for healing. Thank You for keeping me sane in times such as these. I praise your name for the many blessings that many of us take for granted. In Jesus Name! Amen.

Thank You, Lord for giving me a new opportunity to serve you and to uplift my fellow man. I pray that while I am under construction that you will teach me to have patience through the process. Let my light so shine that I may serve as a beacon to one who may be misguided. Keep me humble but teachable all the days of my life. In Jesus Name! Amen.

Thank You Lord for allowing this cracked vessel another opportunity to commune with and serve you. Lord, ask that while you are working on and within me, that you allow me to be a blessing to another. Teach me how to share those gifts and talents you have blessed me with so that I may lead a life void of selfishness. I pray that at the end of this day that all that I have said and done will be pleasing in your sight. In Jesus Name! Amen.

Thank You, Lord for allowing me to see this new day. Let me not focus on my flaws, mistakes and short comings, instead remind me that I am perfectly created vessel filled with your spirit. In Jesus Name! Amen.

Thank You Lord for waking me this morning. Father I pray that you will help me to focus on the number of times I have gotten up and not fallen down. I uplift the sick and their loved ones in prayer today, I pray for healing on their behalf. I pray that those who are fighting the good fight do not give in or give up. Strengthen your children this day that we may resist temptation from the enemy. In Jesus Name! Amen.

Heavenly Father, I rise this morning thanking You that last night's laying down was not my last night. I pray that you would dispatch your angels to deliver healing to the sick. Bless me this day with favor, protection, productivity and growth. In Jesus Name! Amen.

Thank You, Lord for this new day. I pray that you will move in a way that causes us to repent for our sins. Teach us Lord to have patience with our fellow man as you have patience with us. Let us not stray from You Lord, but draw us closer for as times such as these we are in need of your goodness and mercy. In Jesus Name! Amen.

My Father, my God; maker of heaven and earth and all in between. I rise this morning praising your name, I am thankful for the activity of my mind and limbs as well as the breath that fills my lungs. I pray that your grace and mercy follow me like a shadow. My continued prayers go up for the sick and those who care for and love them. In Jesus Name! Amen.

Thank You, Lord for another day. I seek you early this morning before the noise of the day builds and distractions increase and try to steal my focus. I ask this day that you would bring healing to the sick and give comfort and peace to the ones who Love them. I go forward today claiming victory over all things that would serve to stand in the way of a closer more meaningful relationship with you. In Jesus Name! Amen.

Thank You, Lord for granting me this new day. I pray that you will continue to richly bless your children so that we may better complete those tasks you have for us. Let there be peace as we leave our homes, peace on our jobs, healing for the sick and relief for the downtrodden Open our hearts and minds so that we may better recognize your omnipotence. In Jesus Name! Amen.

Thank You, Lord for the many undeserved blessings that you have allowed into my life. I pray that you would continue to cover us and give us direction. Bless us this day that we may draw another to you. Let us not be compromised by location or condition. In Jesus Name! Amen.

Father God thank You for waking us up today. Thank You for being so merciful by giving us another chance to bask in Your glory. Once again, thank You for Your grace, mercy and Your peace. We plead the blood of Your Son, Jesus over our lives. Encourage us to strive to be all that you have created us to be In Jesus Name! Amen.

Thank You for this brand new day; a day not promised to any of us. I pause this morning to get on line with the purpose that you have for my life. I take this time to pray for the young and the old, the sick and the healthy, the rich and the poor. I pray for the ones, who feel lost, left out and otherwise downtrodden this day. I pray for the CEO and the custodial engineer. Give peace on this day and every day. In Jesus Name! Amen.

All praises due to he who is worthy. Thanking You Lord always and in all ways for allowing me to see another day. Thanking you that last night was not my last night and for the comfort of knowing that my best days are ahead of me. I ask that you bless your children so that they may serve to bless another. Heal the sick, comfort the lonely and redirect the misguided. In Jesus Name! Amen

Thank You, Lord for allowing your humble servant the opportunity to enter your presence and say Thank You. Thank You for the breath that inflates my lungs, the movement of my limbs and the activity of my mind. I thank You for seeing past my flaws and loving me the same. I pray that you would find favor with me this day. Let the words of my mouth and the meditation of my heart be acceptable in your sight. In Jesus Name! Amen.

Thank You, Lord for this new day. We thank You for a new opportunity to not only speak to you, but to have you pour into our lives. Show us how to live unselfish lives, giving of ourselves as you have given to us. Bless us this day that we may be all that you have created us to be. In Jesus Name! Amen.

Heavenly Father, I thank You for calling my name and waking me this morning. I go forward this day believing that what you have for me is for ME. Help me to remove all barriers and obstacles that serve to distract me from the true plan you have for my life. I am Thankful for the reminder that prayer is not just about me petitioning you, but more importantly, it's about me listening to You. In Jesus Name! Amen.

Thank You, Lord for filling my nostrils with your breath this morning. I pray for those who did not receive this gift today. I thank You for loving such a perfectly imperfect vessel such as myself. Bless me Lord this day so that I may be a blessing to another. Give me patience with me as I strive to be better and do better day by day. In Jesus Name! Amen.

Thank You, Lord for allowing me to see a new day. I am Thankful that last night was not my last night. I pray that the gifts and talents deposited within me will not become stagnant, but be used to build and uplift my fellow man. I ask your continued blessings upon my life as the lives of all who read this prayer. In Jesus Name! Amen.

Thank You, Lord for allowing my eyes to open and see this new day which you have so graciously granted me. I pray for my fellow man as I do for myself. I pray for healing for the sick and direction for the lost. Replace anxiety and doubt with hope and belief. Protect us from those things that would cause our demise. In Jesus Name! Amen.

Heavenly Father I rise this morning with a mouth full of praise. You woke me up this morning and have ushered me into this new day. I praise your name because your grace and mercy are more than enough. I ask that you would forgive me for my lack of faith, fear and doubt. Bless me Lord so I may bless another. Protect your children from the one whose goal it is to kill, steal and destroy. In Jesus Name. Amen!

Thank You, Lord for bringing me into this new day. I Thank You that last night was not my last night. I pray that you would bless me so that I may share your love with another. I continue to pray for my fellow man as I do myself. Bless the down trodden, depressed, mentally and physically ill. Surround your children with your hedge of protection. In Jesus Name. Amen.

Heavenly Father I enter into your presence this morning thanking You for blessing me to see another day. I send prayers this morning, not for myself but for my fellow man who is experiencing trials and tribulations. The woman I passed this morning who is dealing with depression, the day laborer who is ready to give up and the professional who is battling personal demons. Cover us with your grace and mercy in Jesus Name! Amen.

Thank You, Lord for allowing me to open my eyes, place my feet on the floor, stretch, grunt and groan, all the while praising your name for another day. I praise your name in advance for the opportunities, doors and windows that you will open for me. I thank You for keeping those things from me that would harm or destroy me. Father, continue to feed my faith and starve my doubt. I pray that you would heal the sick and comfort the lonely and misguided. In Jesus Name. Amen!

Heavenly Father I Thank You for the extension of grace and mercy for a cracked and worn vessel such as I. I am forever grateful that you still see fit to bless me day by day. Father, as life does what it does, I pray that you will never remove your hand from my life. Keep me in position to hear from you as well as be used by you for your Glory. In Jesus Name! Amen.

Heavenly Father, I humbly enter into your presence. I kneel at your throne Thanking You for allowing me to be present for this morning's role-call. I bless your name, for your grace and mercy are more than enough. I pray that you would forgive my episodes of worry, fear and doubt. Fill me with your spirit and never let me forget that with You all things are possible. Surround me with your hedge of protection this day. In Jesus Name! Amen

Thank You, Lord for gifting me with a brand new day. I appreciate and receive the blessings that you have in store for me this day. As I go through this day, Lord I ask that you keep your hand on me. Allow me to hear your voice above the noise of life. In Jesus Name! Amen.

Thank You, Lord for last night not being my last night. I am overjoyed that you have seen fit to include me in this morning's roll call. I pray that those things which you have deposited in me will manifest in due time and that I may be able to serve as a light for another. Bless us this day a we leave our homes and travel the airways, highways and byways to our various destinations. Allow us to return home at our appointed time safe from any harm, hurt or danger. In Jesus Name! Amen.

Thank You, Lord for this new opportunity to enter into your presence and worship you. Forgive me for the times that I have been less than faithful to you while you have been more than generous to me. Let my words, thoughts and actions represent whose I am. Let those things which you have deposited within me be used for your Glory. In Jesus Name! Amen.

Almighty God, creator and sustainer of the heavens, the earth and all in between. I rise this morning offering my praise for allowing me to see another day. I Thank You for the trials and tribulations that have caused me to seek you and trust you completely. Let me not gloss over the little blessings and cause myself to truly miss being blessed. Cause me to remember that I am primarily blessed to be a blessing to another. Surround me with your hedge of protection so that no harm, hurt or danger might come my way. In Jesus Name! Amen.

Thank You, Lord for this new day. Thank You for the warm blood that pulses through my veins, as well as the activity of my limbs and my mind. Thank You for allowing me to make mistakes and to learn and grow from the same. I pray that you would continue to draw me closer to you while emptying me of those less desirable traits and filling me with your spirit. I speak blessings to all who acknowledge you as Lord and Savior. In Jesus Name! Amen.

I rise this morning thanking You for Life, breath and mercy. I am grateful for a brand new day, a new opportunity to receive a blessing as well as to be a blessing. I continue to pray for peace and patience. Allow me to lead a life with dignity and humility and never to miss an opportunity to learn from my experiences. In Jesus Name! Amen.

I Give Thanks to the Lord for his bountiful blessings. I pray that you would touch these who are struggling. Help those who are dealing with depression, anxiety and despair uplift them in a way that alerts them that you have not forsaken them. Help those who are struggling financially to stretch their resources, open their eyes to better discern wants from needs. Help us all to be Grateful for what we have and not attempt to try to impress those who do not have our best interest at heart. In Jesus Name! Amen.

Good Morning, Lord, Thank You for your touch that wakes me from my slumber. I praise your name because you continue to be better to me than I deserve. Keep my mind clear from clutter and distractions. Build up my Faith and tear down all doubt. In Jesus Name! Amen.

Heavenly Father I come before you as humbly as I know how. I Thank You for your Grace and Mercy that keeps me. Lord, I need you, I open myself to receive all that you have to deposit within me. I embrace the purpose and plan that you have wonderfully crafted for my life. I pray for guidance, health and strength. I pray that I am a good steward of those things you have trusted me with. In Jesus Name! Amen.

Thank You, Lord for blessing me with this new day. I praise your name because you continue to bless me day after day. I'm breathing, I'm alive and I'm blessed. In Jesus Name! Amen.

I fall to knees this morning thanking You for blessing me with another undeserved day. I am grateful that you still find fit to bless a broken vessel such as I. I pray for those that have as well as those who don't have. I pray that you would remove those things from me that are not pleasing in your sight. Fill me with your spirit and cleanse my soul. Surround you children with your hedge of protection, protecting us from those people and things that would bring us harm, hurt or danger. In Jesus Name! Amen.

I rise this morning praising your name for the bountiful blessings that you have so greatly allowed into my life. I Thank You for finding favor with this broken vessel. I pray that you would continue to bring healing to the sick, uplift to the downtrodden and peace to those who seek it. In Jesus Name! Amen.

Lord, I come before you this morning thanking You for blessing me with another day. I ask that you touch the lives of those who empty themselves of selfish desire and yearn for your spirit to fill them up. I ask that you touch those who are struggling financially. Help them to stretch their resources So that their needs may be met. Lead us far from temptation and cause us to seek your face at all times. In Jesus Name! Amen.

Thank You, Heavenly Father always and in all ways for blessing me to see another day. As we prepare to bring in a "New' year. I pray that you would encourage us to let go and let God. Help us to flee from those things that distract us from those things you would have us to do. Feed our Faith and severely starve our doubt. Send your peace our way because we need it! In Jesus Name! Amen.

Thank You, Lord for this new day. I thank You for bringing me this far. I pray that you would empty me of those things that are not pleasing in your sight. Fill me with your spirit so that I might share it with others. I pray for your continued grace for myself, my family and my friends. In Jesus Name! Amen.

Thank You for your stirring of the spirit that wakes me from my slumber. I pray that as we venture out of our homes this morning for work or leisure that we will do so with your blessings. I pray that your hedge of protection would surround us from the dangers that are ever present. I ask that you bless all in a way that speaks to us individually and lets us know that you are never far from us. In Jesus Name! Amen.

Father God, I want to thank You for who you are and who you continue to be. I thank You for allowing me to see this new day. I ask that you would forgive me of my sins and indiscretions. I pray for healing for the sick, comfort for those who have lost loved ones or who have been displaced by natural disasters. Father God, I ask that you increase my prayer life, add to my compassion and empathy. In Jesus Name! Amen

Thanking You always and in all ways for allowing me to wake this Christmas morning. I pray that as families and friends gather that we don't forget the reason for the season. Let our aim be to live unselfishly and to give generously. In Jesus Name! Amen.

Thank You Lord for safe keeping last night as the storms and winds blew. I pray for those who lost their homes, but thankfully they did not lose their lives. I pray for the families of those who lost loved ones to the storm. Provide them with peace and understanding. Encourage us to remember that what is or is not under the tree is not important, but it is the Love of Christ that matters most. In Jesus Name! Amen.

Heavenly Father, I enter your presence this morning as humbly as I know how. I seek your undeserved grace and mercy. I ask that you would continue to cover and bless your children. Insulate us from the evils that men do. As many prepare to overindulge and over spend, let us not forget those gifts that are given freely by you daily. In Jesus Name! Amen.

Thank You, Lord for last night's slumber and this morning waking up. I declare this day that any plot, plan, or weapon designed by the enemy to knock me off course this day are cancelled! I praise the name of the Almighty God always and in all ways for you are worthy. Grant to me the patience, peace and strength necessary to face those things ahead of me. In Jesus Name! Amen

Thank You, Lord for this new day. Thank You for the warm blood that pulses through my veins, as well as the activity of my limbs and my mind. Thank You for allowing me to make mistakes and to learn and grow from the same. I pray that you would continue to draw me closer to you while emptying me of those less desirable traits and filling me with your spirit. I speak blessings to all who acknowledge you as Lord and Savior. In Jesus Name! Amen.

rise this morning thanking You for Life, breath and mercy. I am grateful for a brand new day, a new opportunity to receive a blessing as well as to be a blessing. I continue to pray for peace and patience. Allow me to lead a life with dignity and humility and never to miss an opportunity to learn from my experiences. In Jesus Name! Amen.

I Give Thanks to the Lord for his bountiful blessings. I pray that you would touch these who are struggling. Help those who are dealing with depression, anxiety and despair uplift them in a way that alerts them that you have not forsaken them. Help those who are struggling financially to stretch their resources, open their eyes to better discern wants from needs. Help us all to be Grateful for what we have and not attempt to try to impress those who do not have our best interest at heart. In Jesus Name! Amen.

I rise this morning extremely grateful that you have given me the beginning of a new day. I pray that I adequately use those gifts and talents that you have deposited within me. I pray this day for those who are dealing with depression. Touch them Lord and remind that they are NOT alone. Surround us with your hedge of protection so that no harm, hurt or danger might come our way. In Jesus Name! Amen.

Thank You, Lord for so richly blessing me this day with my health and sanity. I pray that you would continue to starve my doubt and feed my faith. Let my words, thoughts and actions this day represent the peace and confidence within. Allow me to be a blessing to another today. In Jesus Name! Amen.

Thank You, Lord for the gift of a new day. I Thank You Lord for giving me all that I need and teaching me to work for those things I want. I pray this morning for peace within. Keep your children safe as we leave our homes and travel to our various destinations. Heal the sick and mend the broken. Forgive our doubt, let us not be crippled fear, instead lead us into the promises you have for each of our lives. In Jesus Name! Amen

Heavenly Father, Thank You for last night's laying down and this morning's waking up. I cast all of my cares on you today Lord never to pick them up again. I ask that you forgive my doubt, fear and anxiety and ask that you would remove the same. I send a prayer for ALL people as WE are ALL in need of restoration and healing. In Jesus Name! Amen.

Heavenly Father I Thank You for your touch which lets me know that I am still among the living. I bless your name for the grace and mercy you continue to show me. I pray that you will break the chains that are holding your children hostage. Free us from those things which serve to limit us. Remind us that you have planted greatness in all of us. Help us to see differences as opportunities and not justification for hate, disenfranchisement or alienation. In Jesus Name! Amen.

Thank You, Lord for opening my eyes this morning. I praise your name for the grace and mercy that you have extended my way. I pray that you will move in a mighty way, we need you now Lord always and in all ways. In Jesus Name! Amen.

Thank You Lord for waking me this morning. Heavenly Father allow me to not lose sight of the blessings and promises around me. Keep me positive and hopeful in light of the turmoil, death and destruction that is continuing to show its unsightly face. Protect us from ourselves Lord. In Jesus Name! Amen.

Our Father, our God, creator of heaven and earth and all in between. I rise this morning thanking You for life, movement, sight, mental clarity and another chance. Let not the troubles of the world or the evil that men do cause my faith to waiver. Lord we need you now in a major way. Keep us behind your hedge of protection, draw us one to another. In Jesus Name! Amen.

Heavenly Father As we approach our rest hour, we say thank You for yet another day. Lord as followers and doers of Your Word, we experience the fiery trial and to be honest someday we don't like it. We would rather someone else go thru it but THANK YOU for allowing us to go thru it because Your Love guides us thru and we can't have a testimony without a test. So Lord grant us with peace love and a sound mind and allow us to wake ready to carry out the day. In Jesus Name Amen!

Heavenly Father, I thank You this morning for allowing me to be among the living this day. I praise your name in advance for the blessings that are headed my way. I Thank You for lifting me up the many times I have stumbled and fallen. I Thank You for being my cheerleader when I felt I was on the losing team. Praising your name always and in all ways. In Jesus Name! Amen.

I rise this morning extremely grateful for another chance. A chance not given because it was deserved or even earned. A chance that could not be bought. Another chance that was given because the Lord saw fit to forward me an advance portion of grace and mercy. I pray that my light will so shine today that I may serve as a beacon of hope to another. As I strive to not lean on my own understanding, I will acknowledge the Lord's hand on my life for he shall direct my path. In Jesus Name! Amen.

Thank You for the breath that fills my lungs and the warm blood that flows through my veins. I pray that all I do and say today will be pleasing to your sight. Let me not get ahead of you and your perfect timing. Teach me to be patient and know that you are in control. Allow me to take comfort in knowing that what you have for me is totally for me. I walk in confidence and commit my ways to You Lord. In Jesus Name! Amen.

Thank You, Lord for the many blessings that you have sent my way. I praise your name because your are indeed more than worthy. I am grateful for the undeserved grace and mercy given to me. I pray for peace while in the midst of trials and tribulations. Bless me so that I may be a blessing to another. In Jesus Name! Amen.

Thank You, Lord for your touch that awakens me from my slumber. I praise your name because I am alive! You have given me the control of my limbs and the full ability of my mind. Give me the courage to do what is Good and Just. Lead me away from selfish and otherwise destructive thinking. In Jesus Name. Amen.

Heavenly Father. Thank You for allowing me to see this most Good and Pleasant day. I Thank You for the fellowship. You have allowed me to participate in this last few days. I pray that you would grant traveling mercies to all this day, especially the men Of Omega who are returning home from the Leadership Conference. We love You and we bless your Holy Name. In Jesus Name! Amen.

Lord I Thank You for allowing me to come before you this evening, whole and complete as I was this morning when you saw fit to wake me. Father I Thank You for blessing me this day, Thank You for family, friends and loved ones. Keep my soul in safe keeping this night give me peaceful and restful slumber so I may wake refreshed, renewed and energized. In Jesus Name! Amen.

Heavenly Father. I rise this morning thanking You for an able body and a competent mind. Thank You for being ever present in my life. Let my words and my actions bring honor and glory to your name. Cleanse my heart and soul with your spirit. In Jesus Name! Amen.

Heavenly Father, I thank You for your goodness and mercy. Your daily blessings continue to amaze and humble me. I pray for healing for the sick, strength for the weak and renewed desire to see it through for all. Teach us to live a life of respect for others, giving of ourselves and our talents unselfishly. In Jesus Name! Amen.

I Thank You Lord for blessing me with another day. You have looked beyond my sins and indiscretions and have continued to bless me. I pray that you will keep your hand on my life, allow my valley experiences to grow me and draw me closer to you. Bless those who bless me as well as those who curse me. In Jesus Name! Amen.

Thank You Lord for allowing me to see a new day, a new morning gifted to me to achieve and to grow. I Thank You for providing perfect blessing to one with so many perfect imperfections. I ask that you forgive me of my sins especially those of fear and doubt. I pray that as you continue to work on me and in me that you will starve my doubt and feed my faith. Give me the patience to see it through and the understanding to know that there is a lesson in it all. In Jesus Name! Amen.

I rise this morning with praise on my lips and sincere gratitude in my heart. I thank You for your favor which is given; not based on merit. Father, I ask for patience and peace, I pray that my life, walk and talk bring glory to your name and represent your hand on my life. In Jesus Name! Amen.

Lord I come this morning as humbly as I know how, not asking for anything but to offer my praise and thanks for all that you have done for me. I Thank You for the talents and gifts that you have blessed me with. I thank You for my health and sanity. I Thank You for the healing and restoration that is going on all around me. I bless your name this day and every day. In Jesus Name! Amen.

I come before you this morning with praise on my lips. You woke me up this morning and started me on my way. I Thank You for blessing me with my right mind and full control of my limbs. I pray for healing for the sick, guidance for the misdirected and compassion for the masses. In Jesus Name! Amen.

I rise this morning Thanking You Lord for your continued blessings. I Thank You for last night's slumber and this morning's call to action. I praise your name for allowing me to wake in my right mind. I Thank You for your hand on my life. Heal our hearts and minds and adjust our moral compass so that we may bring your name glory. In Jesus Name! Amen.

Thank You, Lord for the opportunity to be in your presence once again. I humbly come before you with praise upon my lips. I Thank You for the blood that was shed for me, I Thank You for the forgiveness of sins as well as the extension of undeserved grace and mercy toward me. I pray that you would move in a way that would encourage us to live unselfishly and cause us to better treat and respect one another. Let us not stray from your word and its teachings. This is my humble prayer. In Jesus Name! Amen.

Thank You Lord for allowing me to see this new day that you have set forth for I pray that my words and actions this day reflect how blessed I truly am. Go with me this day and every day. I pray that you would protect me from dangers both seen and unseen. In Jesus Name! Amen.

Thank You, Lord for allowing me to wake to see another day. I am grateful for another chance this day. I come this morning standing against sickness and disease. I pray for those that are ill, but also for those who act as caregivers. I pray for their strength spiritual, mental and physical. Lord, in these times of turmoil, I pray that you will move in a mighty way. Let us remember to treat others the we want to be treated. In Jesus Name! Amen.

Thank You, Lord for the opportunity to enter your presence once again. I come humbly to praise your name for this new day. Lord, I pray that you would protect my family, friends and loved ones from hurt, harm or danger. I pray that you would rebuild, restore and strengthen relationships. Father, I ask this day that you would keep your arm around my shoulder and your hand over my mouth until my appointed time to speak. In Jesus Name! Amen.

Thank You, Heavenly Father for allowing me to see another day. I Thank You for the blessing of health, mental, physical and spiritual. I pray this day that you would see fit to keep us from all hurt, harm or danger. I pray for peace in the home and the workplace. Bless is this day so that we may be a blessing to another. In Jesus Name! Amen.

Thank you always and in all ways for life, breath and the many undeserved blessings that have come and are coming my way. I pray that you would continue to cover us with your protection, love, mercy and favor. Bless us this evening as we prepare to slumber and we will be careful to praise your name upon opening our eyes in the morning. I ask that you would forgive us of our sins and heal our mind, body and spirit. In Jesus Name! Amen.

I rise this morning overjoyed that you have seen fit to wake me another day. I praise your name for you are more than worthy. I Thank You for what you have done, what you are doing and the magnificent things yet to come. In Jesus Name! Amen.

I enter into your presence with praise and thanksgiving. Thank You for blessing me in spite of me. As the temperature drops outside, I am thankful for the warmth of my soul that you provide. Bless those who are forced to deal with the current frigid temperatures. In Jesus Name! Amen.

Thank You Lord for allowing me to rise to see this new day. I pray that you will keep me safe from harm, hurt or danger as I strive to complete those things that you would have me to do. Let me not be knocked off course due to petty disagreements, prideful or arrogant behavior. More of you and less of me. In Jesus Name! Amen.

I Thank You Lord for picking me up when I stumble and fall, I Thank You even more for keeping me from those things that would surely cause my demise. Because you allowed me to wake to see another day I know that you still have much more work for me to do. I pray that this cracked vessel will represent your hand on my life for others to see. In Jesus Name! Amen.

Thank You Lord for this new day. I pray for my fellow man as I pray for myself. Teach us to live unselfishly, giving or serving others as you have done for us. Let our true character shine at all times showing the world whose we are. I pray for those experiencing loss at all times, but specifically during this holiday season. Give us peace within. In Jesus Name! Amen

Thank You Lord for bringing me safely to the close of yet another day. I am thankful for the abundance of grace, mercy and blessings that you have allowed to permeate my life. I rest easy this evening knowing that you are with me, and with you no one or nothing can be against me. In Jesus Name! Amen.

Thank You Lord for blessing me this morning by allowing me to wake in my right mind, with full use of my limbs. I am thankful because you continue to see purpose and possibility in this cracked vessel. I continue to pray for peace of mind and clarity of thought as there is still so much tension in the world. Remind us to treat others as we ourselves wish to be treated. In Jesus Name! Amen.

I bow before you this evening for you are worthy of all the praise. I Thank You for keeping me close to you and safe from all harm hurt or danger. I pray that you will continue to extend your Grace and Mercy day by day. I pray that you will keep me and mine safe this night as we slumber. In Jesus Name! Amen

Thank You Lord for allowing me to wake and to partake in this new day. I pray for strength and clarity. I pray for those experiencing loss and separation from loved ones. Protect us from the evils of the world as well as those evils from within. In Jesus Name! Amen.

Thank You Lord for another day. I pray that my dealings this day will be those full of purpose and revelation. I pray that I will be positioned to provide support and uplift to those in need. Let my words and actions consistently reflect whose I am. In Jesus Name! Amen.

Thank You Lord for blessing me with such fullness that you have allowed me to make a difference for another. The sacrifices you have made for me allow me to give freely to others. I pray for comfort for those who are missing loved ones this holiday season. Give them peace and comfort and let them recognize your presence in the midst of it all. In Jesus Name! Amen.

Thank You Lord for blessing me with such fullness that you have allowed me to make a difference for another. The sacrifices you have made for me allow me to give freely to others. I pray for comfort for those who are missing loved ones this holiday season. Give them peace and comfort and let them recognize your presence in the midst of it all. In Jesus Name! Amen.

This evening I come to say Thank You for all you have done for me. I pray that as we enter this Christmas Season that we do not forget that YOU are the reason for the season. I ask that you bless those who are dealing with loneliness, depression and loss of loved ones. In Jesus Name! Amen.

Thank You for opening my eyes to see this new day. My prayer this day and every day is that I will spend my time wisely and purposefully. Lord as you continue to open doors for me I pray for patience and confidence along the way. Use me to be a blessing to another. In Jesus Name! Amen

At the close of this most blessed day I gather my thoughts and offer you praise. I Thank You for loving me and providing unselfishly for me. I pray that you will give your children peace and understanding to deal those injustices and troublesome times associated with this life. In Jesus Name! Amen.

I Thank You Lord for your Grace and Mercy that allows me yet another chance. I pray that you will insulate me from the evils of the world. I ask that You will keep me humble in good times and show me how to act with dignity when faced with adversity. All of me needs all of you. In Jesus Name! Amen

I Thank You Lord for your Grace and Mercy that allows me yet another chance. I pray that you will insulate me from the evils of the world. I ask that You will keep me humble in good times and show me how to act with dignity when faced with adversity. All of me needs all of you. In Jesus Name! Amen

Thank You for filling my nostrils with your breath this morning. I pray that as I leave the peace and tranquility of my home that you will surround me with your hedge of protection. Let my actions speak of my character and my words reflect your hand on my life. In Jesus Name! Amen.

As the evening turns to night I stop to say Thank You for keeping me in spite of me. I pray Dear Lord that you will forgive me of my sins. Draw me closer to thee so that there can be nothing that can separate me from you. Give me the wherewithal to push through times of difficulty and the humility and common sense to recognize that without you I am nothing. Watch over my soul while I rest, so that I might wake recharged and renewed. In Jesus Name! Amen.

All praises do to he who is worthy! Thank You for blessing me with yet another day. I pray for strength, healthy, clarity of thought and divine direction. I pray that my actions today and everyday represent whose I am. In Jesus Name! Amen.

Thank You Lord for your extension of Love, Grace and Mercy towards me. Although I know I have fallen short you have kept those things designed to take me out away from me. As I slumber this evening I pray that you will watch over my family and friends. Keep them from harm, hurt or danger. I ask these things in the name of Jesus! Amen.

I rise this morning Thanking You Dear Lord for allowing me to see another day. I pray for forgiveness of sins and redemption. Give us more of you Lord for we are all in need. Teach us to lead unselfish lives and share the fullness and bounty of the LOVE you have shown us with others. In Jesus Name! Amen

I come this evening as humble as I know how to say Thank You for blessing me. Thank You for your hedge of protection that keeps me safe from day to day. Thank You for caring so deeply for a wretch like me. In Jesus Name! Amen

Thank You for your gentle touch which wakes me from my slumber. I pray that you will help me to take my eyes off of the trials and tribulations of life and make time to look to you. Remind me that I walk by faith always and in all ways and not by sight. Although I cannot see all that you are doing Lord I know that all you are doing is in my best interest. I pray that my good days will continue to outweigh my bad days, and I will do my level best not to complain. In Jesus Name! Amen.

Thank You Lord for allowing me to partake in this most blessed day. I am grateful for the talents and gifts that You have given me and that you have allowed me to share with others. Keep me humble along this journey, living life to the fullest unselfishly. I pray for patience, peace and understanding. In Jesus Name! Amen.

Thank YOU Lord for allowing me to wake from my slumber this morning. Father I ask that You help us to remain faithful through the storm. Let us be part of the solution and not another problem. Let us not abandon ship for fear of sinking, instead help us to focus on you and not be distracted or consumed by our surroundings. In Jesus Name! Amen.

I Thank You Lord for allowing me to rise this morning. I pray that as tensions continue to rise that your peace will spread and increase incrementally. Teach us to treat others as we desire to be treated for we are all wonderfully made in your image. Remind us that our words and actions not only tell the world who we are but more importantly whose we are. In Jesus Name! Amen.

Thank You Lord for allowing me to rise in my right mind with activity in my limbs. We need you now Lord always and in all ways. With so much going on in the world, right, wrong or indifferent your people need a fraction of your peace and a large dose of understanding. Lord I pray that the recent events draw us closer to one another and more importantly, closer to you. In Jesus Name! Amen

I rise this morning thanking thee for your continued grace and mercy. I lift my voice to praise your name for you are more than worthy. I Thank You for saving a wretched cracked vessel such as myself. Lord I pray that you touch and heal those who are sick and those in pain. In Jesus Name! Amen.

I praise your name always and in all ways. I Thank You for this most blessed day. I ask that you give strength to those going through those rough patches associated with life. Lord, I come against cancer in all forms. I pray that you would give purpose to their pain, make their journey one of faith not circumstance. Overwhelm you children with your Love. In Jesus Name. Amen.

I rise this morning praising your name for you are indeed worthy. I praise your name for I know that YOU are the center of my joy. I remain humble because I know I could have less. I will always be grateful because I have had less. I pray that you will continue to keep me and my loved ones behind your hedge of protection. In Jesus Name! Amen.

Heavenly Father, the author and finisher of my life. I praise your name always and in all ways for the outpouring of grace and mercy that is ever present in my life. I am Grateful for the blessings you have seen fit to send my way. I pray this evening for the masses. I pray for health, well being and peace. Teach us to respect one another as we want to be respected. Never let us overlook the value of our fellow man. In Jesus Name! Amen

Thank You Lord for gifting me another day. I am grateful for yet another undeserved chance to worship you. I pray for patience and clarity of thought. Remind me that getting to my place of destiny is NOT a sprint but a marathon, help me to endure. Heighten my hearing and make keen my eyesight so that I may better hear you voice and see what you have for me. In Jesus Name! Amen.

My Father in Heaven, Thank You for allowing me to wake to see a brand new day. I go forward today claiming the victory that is mine. I pray for those without enough as well as those with more than enough. Let my words, thoughts and actions be acceptable in your sight. In Jesus Name! Amen.

Heavenly Father as we officially enter the season of Thanks and Giving, let us not forget that we have a daily reminder of such Every Day that we are able to rise and participate in a new day. Remind us daily to pray without ceasing, walk by faith and not by sight and treat our fellow man as we want to be treated. Protect us from the enemy and our own destructive tendencies. In Jesus Name! Amen

My Father my God I am thankful for the outpouring of grace and mercy. You have seen fit to not only save a wretch like me but to bring me forward to this new day. I want to say Thank You for all that you do and have done for me. On this day of Thanksgiving, and every day, I say Thank You. In Jesus Name! Amen.

Thank You Lord for bringing me to the close of yet another day. I am Thankful that you still find use of this cracked vessel, day by day. I pray for safe travels for those traveling far and near to celebrate with their families. Lord, let us not forget to say "Thank You" always and in all ways for all that you have done. In Jesus Name. Amen

I rise this morning thanking You for allowing me to see this new day. During this Thanksgiving Holiday let us not be consumed with how much we are going to eat but keep us ever reminded of those sacrifices that you have made for us. Cause us to pause and focus on the goodness and mercy that is your love. Let us remember to treat each other as we ourselves want to be treated. In Jesus Name! Amen.

Lord I come this evening asking for your peace to rest with us. The climate is thick and tensions are running high. We need you know like never before. Father teach us to pray one for another. Remind us to pray incessantly in good times and bad times and all times in between. Lord we know you have brought us a long way and we know there is still quite a way for us to go. Let us not be distracted, dismayed or rerouted. Keep us doing those things that have purpose. Remind us always that all life matters. In Jesus Name! Amen

Thank You so much for this new day. In the wake of the sorrow, anxiety, anger and confusion that so many of us feel, remind your children that we are blessed and that you have work for us yet to still do. Let us not be consumed this day with how unjust a thing is, but work diligently to affect positive change. Let us not react and abandon thinking, but react with purpose and guidance. Give us peace from within Lord when all around us is not peaceful. Teach us to love one another as you first loved us. In Jesus Name! Amen.

I Thank You for those things that you have done for me, the bountiful blessings and the sacrifices made for me keep me humble. In light of the internal strife and disappointment felt by so many across the country, I want to pause and pray for peace. Lord I ask that you lend your spirit to your people to offer us direction and to provide balance to our lives. Let our faith not suffer due to the injustice felt by so many. In Jesus Name! Amen

Thank You Lord for keeping me safe. I Thank You for giving to me so much unselfishly. I pray that you will forgive me of my sins and help me to learn how to better myself in spite of. Bless me Lord as I prepare to leave the peace and sanctity of my home. Protect me as I travel the highways and byways of life. In Jesus Name. Amen

Thank You for stopping by and touching my soul this morning. Thank You for the gift of this new day. I appreciate and am humbled by the expression of true Love, compassion and mercy that you have extended my way. My prayer this day is that you will bless us all so that we may bless another. Walk with me Lord through the valley of the shadow of death. In Jesus Name. Amen.

Thank You for your love which has kept me safe from harm, hurt or danger. Thanks You for you spirit that puts my mind at ease and comforts my soul when it is uneasy. I pray for those with enough and those without enough. In Jesus Name. Amen

Thank You Lord for your touch that wakes me from my slumber. The sweet sound of you whispering my name tells me that you still have work for me to do. I go forward this day with my head held high for I know that you are with me. I pray for my family and friends one and the same. I speak peace over the job, finances and family. In Jesus Name! Amen.

Thank You for keeping me safe through the night and allowing me to see this new day. The portion of grace you have extended to me is sufficient enough. A cracked vessel such as I praises your name for the blessings you continue to pour out onto me. I Thank You for the son that shines in me and the sun that shines down on me. In Jesus Name! Amen.

Thank You Lord for this day. I pray that my words and actions were acceptable in your sight this day. If any part of my life this day was not up to par I ask that you would forgive me and help me to grow as a result of the experience. In Jesus Name! Amen.

Thank You Lord for allowing me to wake this morning. I Thank You for giving me a reasonable portion of your grace and mercy. I praise your name for you alone are worthy of all the praise. Lord, I pray that you will help us through our individual struggles allow us to come out better in spite of. In Jesus Name! Amen

Thank You Lord for your touch that calls my soul to attention. Your hand provides comfort and peace to my life removing all anxiety, fear and uncertainty. As the temperatures drop outside I pray that the SON will continue to warm our souls from the inside. I pray a special prayer for Matie Brown, I pray for healing. I pray for her family and loved ones. We know if the doctors can name it, YOU Lord can heal it. In Jesus Name! Amen.

Thank You Lord for finding favor with me today. I pray that my dealings this day properly represented your hand on my life. I ask for forgiveness of any and all sins. Let nothing come between me and thee that would cause distance between us. Protect me from me as well as from the enemy. In Jesus Name! Amen.

Thank You Lord for keeping me safe through the night and allowing me to see another day. I pray Lord that you will teach me how to find joy in the journey. Surround me with your hedge of protection this day. In Jesus Name! Amen.

Thank You Lord for your blessings this day. Your grace and mercy is sufficient for one such as me. Bless my family, friends and loved ones this evening. Protect our mind, body and soul from those things that would serve to do us harm. Give us peace from within. In Jesus Name! Amen.

From the rising of the sun to the going down of the same I will praise your name. I praise your name for you are worthy. Where I am, YOU brought me, what I know, YOU taught me. I go forward with confidence this day knowing that what you have for me is for me. I pray that you will teach us to cast our burdens onto you and concern ourselves with those things we can change. In Jesus Name! Amen.

Thank You Lord for calling my name this morning. I pray that your peace will saturate my home, my work place and my life. Let my heart not be troubled by things I cannot control, but find comfort in knowing the author and finisher. Let my existence reflect your blessed hand on my   life.   In   Jesus   Name!   Amen.

Thank You for your many blessings which encompass my life. Thank You for not only sparing my life but holding back the consequences of my disobedience. As this day comes to a close I pray you will give my heart, mind and soul peace. Allow me to wake refreshed and renewed. In Jesus Name! Amen.

Thank You Lord for allowing me to see another day. Lord we ask for forgiveness of our sins. Teach us to love one another as you have first loved us. Teach us to be of help to one another and not serve as a hindrance. Thank You for the Son that shines in us and the sun that shines down upon   us.   Bless   us   this   day   and   every   day.   In   Jesus   Name!   Amen.

Thank You Lord for allowing me to see another day. I pray that you will give me the courage to do what is right, the confidence to see it through and the strength of character to remain humble yet teachable. Bless us so that we may be a blessing. In Jesus Name! Amen.

Thank You Lord for including my name in this morning's role call. I go forward this new day you have blessed me with knowing that no weapon formed against me will prosper. I declare that I am a progressive and productive person. I claim victory over the enemy not only for me but for those I interact with this day. In Jesus Name. Amen.

Thank You Lord for this day. Thank you for the new revelations and opportunities that have come into view. I pray that you will continue to bless me so that I may richly bless another. I pray for peace this evening as I am physically and mentally spent. Watch over my household this evening and we will be sure to give you all the praise. In Jesus Name! Amen.

Thank You Lord for This new day filled with promise and hope. My prayer is that you will fill this cracked vessel and send a blessing through me. Let my attitude be one of gratitude. Help me to resist those things that will attempt to knock me out of position. Hold my hand Lord. In Jesus Name! Amen.

I come this evening on bended knee praising your name always and in All Ways for the extension of grace and mercy that you have shown towards me. I pray that you would dispatch your angels this evening to watch over my friends and loved ones. Let us not further separate ourselves one from another due to political or party affiliation. Draw us one to another as children of the most high. In Jesus Name! Amen.

Thank You Lord for this new day. I Thank You for the unconditional love that you continue to show. I pray that you will continue to feed my faith and starve my doubt. Let the words of my mouth and the meditation of my heart be acceptable in your sight Lord. Let my character speak not for who I am but whose I am. In Jesus Name! Amen.

Thank You Lord for seeing me to the close of this day. I Thank You for allowing me to be a continued part of your plan. Bless your children this evening. Hide us behind your hedge of protection. Let our faith guide us going forward to places our eyes cannot see. Give us the patience and resolve to see all things done to completion. I'm Jesus Name! Amen

I rise this morning thanking You for the movement of my limbs and the activity of my mind. My attitude is that of gratitude. This day I choose to look forward at what is and the possibilities ahead of me and not behind at what was or what could have been. I bless your name Lord because of who you are. I operate in the positive and walk by faith. In Jesus Name! Amen.

Thank You for the extension of your love to a cracked vessel such as myself. I am humbled that in spite of me you still continue to bless me. I ask that you give me the patience and the tenacity to do the work that you have for me. Bless those that bless me as well as those that have other thoughts concerning me. In Jesus Name! Amen

I praise your name always and in all ways for blessing me on the days that end in "y". As I pray Lord, I ask that you slow me down enough to listen to your voice and to receive the answer and direction. Watch over my family and loved ones. Thank You for giving me those things I need and showing me how to work for those things that I want. I entrust my mind, body and spirit to you this evening for protection in Jesus Name. Amen.

Heavenly Father, I rise this morning thanking You for touching my soul. I wake knowing that when I cast all my cares upon you that they will trouble me no more. I pray that you will comfort those in distress and guide the misdirected. Encourage us to go above and beyond ourselves, unlocking   our   hidden   potential.   In   Jesus   Name!   Amen.

I come this evening Lord not wanting to let another minute pass without your humble servant pausing to give you Thanks for the battles you have helped me to overcome this day. Thank You for opening my eyes to see the opportunities that you have so carefully put into place for me. In Jesus Name! Amen.

I give Thanks Always and in All ways for being afforded yet another opportunity to be counted among the living. My spirit is excited by your touch which stirred me to action this morning. Lord I pray for the confidence and the competence necessary to complete the tasks that are before me today. I pray for patience this day not only when dealing with my fellow man, but when dealing with me. In Jesus Name! Amen.

Thank You for this day Lord. I pray you watch over our souls while we sleep this evening. A special prayer I say today for the 2 little girls who learned of their beloved mothers passing this afternoon. Please Lord comfort the family and give them some level of understanding. In Jesus Name. Amen.

Thank You Lord for your firm but tender hand upon my life. I give you all of the praise for the unselfish and unconditional love that you continue to show me. Bless my loved ones, family and friends as we prepare to slumber this evening. More of You and less of me, that is my prayer. In Jesus Name! Amen.

Thank You Lord for giving me the gift of a new day. Thank You for continually looking past my faults and continuing to bless me. Strengthen me from within Lord as this journey of life has its hills and valleys. To See it Through is the only thing I know. In Jesus Name! Amen.

Thank You Lord for another unpromised day. Thank You for remembering to bless me when I neglect to Thank You. Fill me with your anointing this day so that I don't run low. Give me the courage and resolve to do those things that are right and often times difficult. Let your light so shine in me this day that I blind the enemy and serve as a beacon, lighting the way for the misguided. In Jesus Name! Amen.

Thank You for this day and the blessings therein. Thank You for not pulling your hand away from me when I was disobedient or got ahead of you. Slow me down so that I may hear your voice that much better. In Jesus Name! Amen.

I rise this morning with a sense of promise and praise. I am excited about those things that are before me this day. I pray that I learn to not be consumed with complaining about what I don't have and what is wrong in my life, instead let me rejoice in the blessings that you have so gracefully sent my way. Let my attitude be one of gratitude. Walk with me and talk with me. Let my posture and response this day not only show the world who I am, but whose I am. In Jesus Name! Amen

I pause at this very moment to acknowledge your hand on my life. I Thank You for the blessings you have afforded me this day. I ask that you would keep my friends and loved ones safe this evening. More of you and less of me Lord, that is my prayer. In Jesus name! Amen.

Thank You for the precious gift of life. I Thank You all ways and in all ways for blessing one such as me. This cracked vessel is ready to be filled and used for your glory. Let me not be limited due to my surroundings but flourish in spite of my surrounds. In Jesus Name! Amen.

Thank You, Lord for waking me this morning. I pray for peace within as I go about this day. Give me patience as I continue to deal with the things that life sends my way. Let me not lose sight or be detoured from the path that is before me. In Jesus name! Amen.

I come this evening as humbly as I know how to say Thank You for continuing to bless me in spite of me. I ask that you forgive me of my sins. Protect me from me and the danger all around me. Bless those who bless me and those who do otherwise. Teach me how to treat others better than they treat me. Let me be the change I want to see. In Jesus name! Amen.

Heavenly Father I rise this morning giving you all the praise. I pray today Lord that you will strengthen your children spiritually, emotionally and above all morally. Let us not set aside those things that define our character in an attempt to fit in. Let us be the light that you have designed us to be. I pray that you will continue to bless us all individually and collectively for the greater good. In Jesus Name! Amen.

I pray this evening for peace of mind in the midst of the trouble we all face day to day. I come this evening leaning on your word, and although I don't know your plans, I do know who made the plan. I put my hand in your hand this evening and continue to seek a closer walk with You. In Jesus Name! Amen.

I lift my eyes unto the hills from whence comes my Help. I Thank You Lord for being the one constant in my life they neither wavers nor has failed me. Draw me nearer to You Lord. As the country is in the midst of a major health concern, I just ask that your will be done, in all things. In Jesus Name! Amen.

I Thank You Lord for allowing me to make it to the close of this day. I ask for nothing more than for you to protect my soul while I slumber. Keep my family and loved ones safe from harm, hurt or danger. Bless us Lord individually and collectively. Remind us that when we bring a burden to you that we are to leave it there, never to pick it up again. In Jesus Name! Amen.

Thank You for safe passage through the winds and storms that affected many of us last night. We bless your name for you are worthy of all the praise. We Love you Lord. We need you always and in All Ways. In Jesus Name! Amen.

Thank You for waking me this morning. Your faithfulness encourages me to push harder and to learn to love myself and my fellow man that much more. Let my words and actions represent that of a child of the one true God. In Jesus Name! Amen.

Thank You, Lord for waking me this morning. I pray that as I go into this day that I will show the world whose i am. Let my word and actions properly represent your hand on my life. Remind us that when we put our problems in your hands that you place your peace upon our hearts. In Jesus Name! Amen.

Amidst the activity of this day, I pause to say Thank You and to praise your name. Lord, I pray for the strength to go on when I am tired and the courage to see it through when the odds seem to be against me. Give me peace of mind, body and soul. Allow me to wake refreshed and eager to do your will. In Jesus Name! Amen.

Heavenly Father, I Thank you for keeping me through the night and allowing me to rise this morning. I give you all the praise for you are indeed worthy. I leave yesterday's burdens with you never to revisit them again. I go forward praising your name and claiming victory. In Jesus Name! Amen.

From the rising of the sun to the going down of the same, I will praise your name. You continue to bless me far beyond what I deserve. Your Grace and Mercy is sufficient. Bless me this evening by giving me peace of mind, body and spirit. Allow me to rise in the morning refreshed and reset for a new day. In Jesus Name! Amen.

I rise this morning thanking You for sparing my life and allowing me to see yet another day. I pray that you will go before and with me this day. I Thank You in Advance for those things which you are doing in my life. In Jesus Name! Amen.

As the moon travels across the sky, I pause to reflect on how good you are and have been to me. I Thank You for your continued hand on my life. I pray that you will keep me from all harm hurt and danger. Bless my family in a mighty way. Surround them with your hedge of protection. In Jesus Name! Amen.

I rise this morning praising the name of My Lord, My God, My Heavenly Father. I give you all the glory and the praise because of who you are and the things you have done and continue to do In my life. I pray for those who are lost, misdirected or otherwise disenfranchised. Your children need you know, Always and in All Ways. In Jesus Name! Amen.

Thank You, Lord for you everlasting Grace and Mercy. Thank YOU for allowing me to see another day. I come only to say Thank You. I desire to do your will this day and every day. In Jesus Name! Amen.

Thank you for your touch which gently wakes me from my slumber. I ask that you continue to keep me in spite of me. I pray this morning for those who are ill and for those who are hurting as a result of losing loved ones. I ask that you give us some degree of understanding followed by a whole lot of peace. We your children need you now like never before. In Jesus Name! Amen

Thank You Lord for bringing me safely to the close of yet another day. I pray Lord that I am operating in your will. Lord if those things I am doing, desiring or planning are not in your will, please let them pass me by and fill me with peace so I that I don't worry about them. Bless us Lord, protect us from those things that will harm us and cause distress. Comfort those that are hurting and redirect those who have lost their way. In Jesus Name! Amen

Thank You Lord for allowing me to rise this morning and to partake in this new and blessed day that you have set in motion. Lord, I pray that I will use my time and talents to uplift another. Please do not allow me to be knocked out of position as a result of the stress and strains of life. Let the words of my mouth and the meditations of my heart be acceptable in thy sight. In Jesus Name! Amen

Heavenly Father, I Thank You for keeping me physically safe, mentally prepared, and spiritually sound. I pray that I will learn and grow from both mistakes and triumph. Slow me down so I can better hear your voice and feel your hand on my life. In Jesus Name! Amen.

Thank You Lord for blessing me life and breath. Thank You for the never ending Love that you show me even when I am disobedient. I go forward this day ready to meet the obstacles in my way squarely face to face. I give you all the praise in advance of those things which I will conquer and overcome this day. In Jesus Name! Amen.

Thank You Lord for allowing me to see yet another day. I pray that you will sharpen my hearing so that I may hear your voice more clearly. Clear my mind so I may not be distracted by those things designed to cause me to lose focus. Let my words, my thoughts and actions show others and remind me of not only who I am, but more importantly whose I am. In Jesus Name! Amen

Father, My God, I wake this morning feeling blessed for I know that You are the author and finisher of my life. I am comforted in knowing that with your hand ever present on my life that no weapon formed against me shall prosper. Dear Lord I need you this day and every day. Without you I am lost. Fill me with your spirit so that I may do your will. Protect me from those things that would do me harm. Please be patient with me. In Jesus Name! Amen.

I rise this morning Thanking You for allowing me to see another today, to rise in my right mind with complete control of my mind and my limbs. I pray this day for peace and clarity of thought. In Jesus Name! Amen.

Thank You for blessing me to see this new day. Let my words and thoughts be pleasing in your sight. Teach me to not hold grudges or ill will toward my fellow man. Instead show me how to grow from the experience and move on. Go with me this day. Strengthen me when I get weak, redirect me when I veer off course and bring me safely to the close of this day. In Jesus Name! Amen.

Heavenly Father, Thank You for the unconditional Love you show me. I thank You for your hedge of protection which keeps me free from harm, hurt or danger. I pray that you will bless my family and friends as you have and continue to bless me. In Jesus Name! Amen.

I Thank You Lord for allowing me the opportunity to see yet another day. The favor you have shown and continue to show me is more than I deserve. Lord, I pray that you will give me the strength to overcome all that comes my way this day. Allow me to rise above those things aimed to bring me down. Keep me humble while going through these and keep me teachable regardless of my station in life. I speak peace and blessings to all. In Jesus Name! Amen.

Heavenly Father, all praises due to you, for you are indeed worthy. You woke me this morning and provided me the tools necessary to be successful and effective this day. You have kept me safe and sane throughout life's ups and downs. I pray that you usher me to slumber this evening with peace. Allow me to wake refreshed mentally, physically and spiritually. In Jesus Name! Amen.

Heavenly Father to whom I owe all that I am, all that I have and all that I know. I offer my humble praise this morning for allowing me to be counted among the living this morning. I pray that I will speak life into situations and uplift those I come into contact with. Help me to live a life unselfishly as you continue to provide and graciously give to me. In Jesus Name! Amen.

I rise this morning with purpose and praise! I Thank You for ushering me into this new day. I pray that as I go forward that you will use me for your glory. Strengthen me so that I may resist those things designed to bring me down or alter my path. Guide me so that when the road ahead looks dark and dangerous I will walk in Faith and not by sight. In Jesus Name! Amen.

Thank You Lord for your continued grace and mercy. Go with me this day, give me the strength and resolve to overcome those obstacles in my way. Make me resistant to the enemy's plans to separate me from you. Make me resilient so that I do not become easily defeated or knocked out of position. Fill me with your spirit. In Jesus Name! Amen.

Thank You Lord every day for your blessings that continue to permeate my life. I am ever so thankful that the master has chosen to not leave me on the shelf, but to use this cracked, perfectly imperfect vessel for your perfect purpose. Bless my going and coming and all in between. In Jesus Name! Amen

Thank You Lord for protecting me from what I thought I wanted and blessing me with what I did not know I needed. Help me to not be led astray or let down by what others say or do to me. Help me to remember that YOU have deposited greatness within me. Give me peace within and around me this night. In Jesus Name! Amen.

Thank You for blessing me so richly to see yet another day. I pray that I will use those gifts and talents given to me to help another and better myself. I Thank You for the sun and the rain, both the same, I pray that I will learn to see the benefit in both and allow myself to grow accordingly. In Jesus Name! Amen

I enter into your presence this evening as humbly as I know how. I Thank You for the many blessings that enhance my life day by day. Bless us all great and small. Send a blessing to me so that you so that you can get a blessing through me. In Jesus Name! Amen.

Thank You for not only bringing us to this new day, but to this last Friday of the year. We come to say Thank You for bringing us this far and for never leaving or forsaking us. We pray for the families of those who did not make it this far this year. We ask that you move on our behalf individually and collectively, strengthening us along the way. Let us now touch and agree and know with all faith that you are there and already working on our behalf. In Jesus Name. Amen!

Good evening Lord. Thank You for the lessons and the blessings intertwined in this day. Thank You for keeping your hand on my life providing for and protecting me from the evils that men do. Help me not lose sight due to the obstacles, but to keep my eyes focused on you. In Jesus Name. Amen!

Heavenly Father, I come before you this morning Thanking You for this new day. I walk forward with my head held high and my arms open ready to receive the blessings that you have in store for me. I pray for the safety of family and friends both near and far. I pray for those who are dealing with depression and loneliness. I come against this spirit sent to separate and destroy. Draw us all closer to you! Be with us as we pray one for another. In Jesus Name. Amen!

All praise due to him who is the author and finisher of my faith. I Thank You for blessing me to not only see but to be a part of this day. I pray that my thoughts, words and actions today have been acceptable in your sight. I pray that my existence has not and will not be in vain but instead will positively affect and bless another. Teach me how to move on from disappointments and not be bitter or spiteful. Build me up so that I am not angered or agitated by those who speak untruths about me. Guard my soul from the attacks of the enemy. In Jesus Name. Amen!

I rise this morning thanking you for the chance to see another day and walk and talk with you. Father I pray for those dealing with loss and depression, insulate their hearts and minds against the tricks of the enemy. Let not what we think we see/hear serve to separate us from your loving touch and your hedge of protection. Speak to us in a form and fashion that we can understand. Walk with us in the valley and along the still waters. Praising your name now henceforth and forevermore. In Jesus Name. Amen!

I bless you Lord for filling my lungs with your breath. THANK YOU for giving me yet another day complete with renewed mercy. Each and every day I yearn to walk closer with you. Teach me to be strong, but not rude. Be kind but not weak. Act purposefully but not recklessly. Continue to work on me and teach me to have patience with me day by day. In Jesus Name. Amen!

At the close of this day that you have blessed me with, I offer Thanks. Let me not be dismayed or disillusioned with the ups and downs of life, instead show me how to be happy for the opportunity of the experience. Walk with me Lord, hold my hand when I drag my feet and dust me off when I stumble and fall. In Jesus Name. Amen!

I rise this morning anxious to greet you Lord. Thank You for the peace of mind that allows my body to rest. I pray that my words, my thoughts and my actions properly represent not only who I am but whose I am. Go before me this day, allow me to make positive deposits into the lives of those less fortunate. Cover my mind so as not to be discouraged or disillusioned by the enemy so that I am not led astray. In Jesus Name. Amen!

Dear Lord, I come this evening on bent knee praising your name for the outpouring of your goodness and mercy. I Thank You for those trials and tribulations that have made me stronger and taught me to seek you with more intensity. I leave my current burdens with you Lord never to pick them up again. Stir my spirit and mold my character. In Jesus Name. Amen!

Thank You for stirring my soul and filling my lungs with your breath. I acknowledge your presence in my life and Thank You for such. My prayer this day is for blessings for all. Let not our Joy be sidelined by the enemy. Teach us to rejoice at all times knowing that YOU are the author and finisher. Teach us to not lean on our own understanding, but to always acknowledge YOU as the head of our lives. In Jesus Name. Amen!

My Father, My God I want to borrow a few minutes of your time just to say Thank You. Not to ask for anything, I just want to say Thank You. Not because of the raise, the house or the job, just want to say Thank You. Not for being the lawyer when I needed one, the doctor when my health was bad or the mental health professional when the voices got loud and out of control. I just want to say Thank You! Thank You for the blessings I deserve, but more so for the multitude of blessings I don't deserve. Thank You for thinking about me when I cared less about anything else. Lord, if you do nothing else, I Thank You. I humbly close with a heartfelt Thank You. Amen!

My Lord, My God. Thank You for last night's slumber and this morning's call to order, Thank You for blessing me with another day. Teach us to appreciate the blessings we have received both great and small. Direct us toward a life filled with positives and show us how to share the love you have shown us with one another. I ask that you lead my steps while in the storm, headed into the storm and out of the storm. In Jesus Name. Amen!

My Creator, Thank You for handling those things which I cannot wrap my arms or my mind around. Teach me to lean not unto my own understanding, as it is flawed tainted and subject to emotion, instead direct my path directly ad I recognize your hand on my life. I acknowledge that I am wonderfully and uniquely designed and ask that you speak to my heart and show me the plan that you have for my life. In Jesus Name. Amen!

Thank You for waking me to see this powerful new day that you have so graciously allowed me to be a part of. I go forward, knowing that the things that trouble me are already done. I do not revisit those burdens which I have left with you. I walk in faith knowing that it is already done. I know that your ways and thoughts are not like my own. I pray for peace, patience and understanding. Let my light so shine that it may serve to positively affect another. This is my humble prayer. Amen!

The Lord is my shepherd, I shall not want. I Thank You for ushering me to the close of this day. I bring that which is currently burdening me this day to you Lord, never to pick it up again. I know that if I trust and do not doubt that all things will work out. Over feed my faith now Lord. Give me peace of mind and a calm, eased spirit. In Jesus Name. Amen!

I rise this morning to kneel before your throne to Thank You for allowing me to see another day. Thank You Lord for your word which serves as the user's manual for my life. Surround me with your hedge of protection today, protect me from me. In Jesus Name. Amen!

Thank You Lord for this new day! Your grace and mercy in spite of my flaws is worthy to be praised. I hold tightly on to YOUR unchanging hand. Father we come asking for Forgiveness for second guessing your plans and direction of our lives. We ask for YOUR Favor over our lives. I pray for those experiencing loss, provide healing of mind, body and spirit. In Jesus Name we Pray. Amen!

Father in Heaven. I come before you this evening feeling blessed and highly favored. With so much to be Thankful for, I can't understand why I let fear and confusion play such a powerful role in my life. Day by day Lord, feed my faith and starve my doubt. Teach me to not look at where I am, but to focus ahead to where I am going. I ask that you give me peace within so that I can grow in you undeterred and unobstructed. In Jesus Name. Amen!

The Lord is my shepherd, I shall NOT want. As you lead me beside the still waters help me to not fret when the waves become a little choppy. Help me to learn to not be overcome with anxiety and uneasiness, instead remind me that I walk by faith and not by sight. Grant me the courage to overcome those things that have me convinced that I cannot. Remind me that MY God is bigger than any scenario that mind can conjure. I proclaim today that I will speak to my giants this day and loudly and proudly proclaim that, I AM A GIANT SLAYER! In the Mighty and Matchless Name of Jesus. Amen!

My Father, creator of Heaven and Earth and all in between. I Thank You for your grace and mercy that allows me to participate in this new day. Father, I ask that you not let me not be worn down by the physical and mental demands of this day. Keep me spiritually strong when I am at my lowest and forever humble when I am at my highest. In Jesus Name. Amen!

My Father, creator of Heaven and Earth and all in between. I Thank You for your grace and mercy that allows me to participate in this new day. Father, I ask that you not let me not be worn down by the physical and mental demands of this day. Keep me spiritually strong when I am at my lowest and forever humble when I am at my highest. In Jesus Name. Amen!

Thank You for waking me this morning and exhaling your breath into my lungs. I ask that you protect me from dangers seen and unseen this day. Watch over my family and loved ones day to day. Thank you for working those things out that I have learned to let go of. Teach me how to let go of those things that I am either afraid to or unwilling to let go of. Speak to me Lord, make your voice louder than the distractions that are all around me. In Jesus Name. Amen!

Lord I come before you this evening as humble as I know how. Not to ask for a single thing, but instead to give you honor and praise for all that you have done and are doing for me. Thank You for the protection that your Love provides. Thanking You with the full totality of my being. In Jesus Name. Amen!

My Father My God Thank You for including my name on your roll call this morning. I rise this morning full of enthusiasm ready to meet today's chores head on. I pray your blessings on my family and friends, meet us were we are, provide us with the means to meet our responsibilities and speak to us so that we can understand. Show us the error of our ways and teach us how to correct them and then grow from them. We ask these blessings in the name of Jesus. Amen!

Thank You Lord for allowing me to see the 1st Sunday of the last month of the year. I am blessed to have been able to share in communion with other believers on this day. Thank you for being a God of another chance when situations and circumstances would have denied me such. Bless me now Lord as I prepare to reboot and recharge for the coming week. Give me peace so that I may rest peacefully until you whisper my name in the morning. In Jesus Name. Amen!

All praise due to he who is worthy. This evening I offer praise always and in all ways for the time, patience and love that you have and continue to show me. I ask your blessings this evening as I slumber. Keep me mentally awake, physically strong and spiritually fortified. In Jesus Name. Amen!

Thank You Lord for allowing me another chance to get it right. I want nothing more this evening than to say "Thank You". Keep me humble enough to know that I am not better than any one person, but wise enough to realize that I am different from the rest. In Jesus Name. Amen!

As I wake from my slumber, I anxiously greet you this morning Lord. I offer to you, my full praise, Thanking You for another day. You did not have to do it, but you did, over and over again. As we prepare to give thanks, let us remember to first Thank You for your sacrifice and your constant grace and mercy that is extended to us day after day, time after time. Let us not forget those who are less fortunate than ourselves. In Jesus Name. Amen!

As we pause this evening to offer our sincere Thank You for allowing us to not only see the rising of the sun but also the going down of the same. As we prepare to gather and give thanks around the table tomorrow, we cannot forget to give thanks for the many blessings that you have allowed to permeate our lives. Let us not forget those that are less fortunate than ourselves, those without any, and those without enough. Encourage us to live lives less selfish, encourage us to pray and toil for one another. Release your spirit to come forth and eradicate the spirit of depression. Wrap your arms around your children hold us safely and tightly in your arms. In Jesus Name. Amen!

Thank You Lord for your bountiful blessings that encompass every part of my life and being. Be with your children now Lord, protect us from the physical, mental and spiritual attacks of the enemy. I come against the spirit of depression which always rears its ugly head during this season of Thanks. Encourage us to not do those things which could separate us from you, but to do those things which ultimately draw us closer to you. I pray for traveling mercies for those traveling to be with family and loved ones. In Jesus Name. Amen !

As this day comes to a close, I stop to reflect on your goodness, mercy and favor. Thank You for allowing me this day to make deposits into the lives of others. Please continue to watch over and guide me along the way. As the temperatures drop outside, I pray for those without adequate heating and more so for those without a place to call their own. Open our hearts so that we may lead less selfish less self centered lives. In Jesus Name ! AMEN

Thank You Lord for ushering me into this new day. I pray that you will give to me the mental toughness to remain strong in spite of....I pray for those who are experiencing loss through death or distance. Be with those who are dealing with depression. Strengthen them and make your presence known in their lives. Do for us that which we cannot do for ourselves, meet us where we are and talk with us in a fashion where we can understand. In Jesus Name. Amen!

My Father, My Lord creator of the heavens and the earth and all In between. I approach this new day with new vigilance, vigor and outlook. I Thank You for reminding me whose I am and more importantly, who I am with you. Go with me Lord this day making my feet keen along this journey. Keep me spiritually full, physically sound and mentally awake. Lead me not into temptation, but deliver me from evil. In the Mighty and Matchless Name of Jesus. Amen!

My Father in Heaven. Thank You for allowing me to wake this day, giving me yet another opportunity to be fed in the House of the Lord. Thank You for the events of this day that continue to show me not only your power and goodness, but also your mercy. Bless me now this evening and forevermore. I pray for the sick and shut in. I come against the spirit of depression during this holiday season. Comfort the uneasy and strengthen the weary. In Jesus Name. Amen!

Heavenly Father, thank You for Your promise of peace. Today, I open my heart to You and ask that You teach me to hear Your voice clearly. I will listen, I will obey, and I will walk in Your ways, in Jesus' name. Amen!

Father in heaven, thank You for sending Your Son, Jesus, to show me the way. I receive Your truth and commit my heart to You. I invite You into every area of my being and choose to follow You all the days of my life, in Jesus' name! Amen.

Thank You Lord for welcoming me to this new day. Your unselfish love shown to me is incomprehensible. You continue to amaze by finding use for one such as me. I am ever grateful for the lessons learned as a result of the trials and tribulations you have allowed me to come through. Never remove your hand from my life. As I go through this day I will do so with confidence, resting on your word. Jesus Name. Amen!

My Lord, My God, to whom all praise is do. I enter into your presence as humbly as I know how, on bended knee with my head bowed. I Thank You for your grace and mercy which keeps me physically fit, mentally sound and spiritually grounded. Grant me your peace this evening as I debrief from the events of this day. Let me not carry old baggage into the new day not promised, but dearly desired. In Jesus Name. Amen!

As the sun makes it's commute across the sky, I praise your name for your awesome display of Love and Power. Grant me the peace and understanding to accept the things that I cannot change, but the resolve to work diligently to positively affect those things that I can. I pray that you will meet and attend to your children in their current situations. Let my light so shine that I may serve as a ray of hope for another. In Jesus Name. Amen!

Thank You for this day. Thank You for your word which is a rock under my feet when times are rough, the light at the end of the tunnel when all around me is dark, the hand that lifts me up when I stumble and fall. Thank You for giving me purpose and passion fueled with massive enthusiasm. Go with me when all others desert me. Protect my family and loved ones as we slumber. Jesus Name. Amen!

Greetings to him who is the author and finisher of my faith. The one who holds the world and all of the richness contained in it. I Thank You for the blessings that you have lined up for me. I pray this day that I will not only be encouraged but also encourage another. Move me from an existence of selfishness to a life of selflessness. In Jesus Name. Amen!

I approach your throne this evening with thanks and praise in my mouth. Thank you for keeping me out of harm's way on this day. I pray that the abundance of your love and favor know no end during my lifetime. Bless my friends and family, bless those who bless me as well as those who plot against me. In Jesus Name. Amen!

Thank You God for calling my name and causing me to answer the role. I pray that I will make good use of my time, gifts and talents this day. Encourage me to go beyond the limitations that man has set for me. Help me to believe in me and my abilities at least a fraction of what you see and believe in me. Give me the strength to carry on when the road becomes an incline with twists, turns and potholes and the weather is suspect at best. In Jesus Name. Amen!

As I rise this morning. I behold the beauty of this new day. I inhale peace, serenity and power and exhale enthusiasm and purpose. I ask for your blessings in all endeavors undertaken today. Help me to make meaningful deposits in the lives of my fellow man. Move me into position to receive what is mine. Do not let my words, actions and deeds block my blessings or create distance between me and you. In Jesus Name. Amen!

Father, this evening, we enter into your presence with humility and Thanksgiving praising your name for the mercy you have shown us and the favor you have afforded us. Bless us this evening as we prepare to slumber, never letting us be separated from you. Dispatch your angels to protect us so that we may wake unharmed and rested in the morning. We ask your blessings this evening and forever more. In Jesus Name we do pray. Amen!

As I rise from my slumber, I do so with a mouth full of praise, a heart running over with thanks, a willing spirit and an able body. Go with me today, Lord, fill me with what I am lacking and reinforce what is already there. Lord as you continue to pass out blessings, please don't forget about me and those that pray with me and for me. In Jesus Name. Amen!

Thank You Lord for bringing me to the close of this day. I know that the events of this day will later serve as my testimony, even though right now, the light and the end of the tunnel appears to be dim. Help me not to become bitter, distant or angry when things don't go the way I want or think they should go, teach me to lean not unto my own understanding, but at all times to acknowledge you. Keep me steadfast, holding on to your hand through thick and thin. Guide me when I am headstrong, pushing, pulling and prodding as needed. We need you more now than ever. In Jesus Name. Amen!

Good Morning Lord! Thank You for calling my name and touching my soul this morning. I pray that the breath you have blown into my nostrils this day will be exhaled with purpose and expectations. I pray for peace within and enough compassion to go around. I pray for my fellow man and I pray that in turn they will pray for me. In Jesus Name. Amen!

Heavenly Father, Thank You for allowing me to be a part of this most awesome day. Thank You for keeping me humble and teachable throughout this journey called life. Thanks for not giving up on me when I did not see nor attempt to live up to my fullest potential. I ask Lord that you continue to bless my life in such a way that I can make meaningful deposits into the lives others. In Jesus Name. Amen!

I rise this morning giving Thanks for allowing me to partake in this new day. Thank You for giving me peace of mind, a strong will to succeed and the tools necessary to do all things through you. I pray for peace and prosperity. I claim healing for the sick, injured and downtrodden. I pray for strength for the weary and comfort and guidance for the misdirected. In Jesus Name. Amen!

All praise is due to him who is worthy. My Lord, My God I Thank You for protecting me from the dangers of the world, the enemy and me. I pray for continued strength and durability of character in all things. Make my ears keen to your voice and my soul sensitive to your touch. Bless me this evening, dispatch your angels to watch over my household and that of my family and friends. In Jesus Name. Amen!

Heavenly Father, this day and every day I pause to say Thank You. I humbly request that you order my steps, help me to put my best foot forward so that I might learn to walk with expectancy, guided by faith and not by sight! Sharpen my ear to your voice so that I am able to be where you want me to be so that I am in position to receive my blessings. I put ALL my trust in you. In Jesus Name. Amen!

Thank You for filling me with your breath so that I might in return exhale destiny. Teach me how to not only embrace my current season, but to learn while in it. Help me to carry over those lessons from season to season so that when my time comes I am prepared and in position. Keep me from fighting the process but to view it as on the job training. Open my eyes so that I might find value in every step along the way. Give me the courage to rise, the perseverance to continue in spite of and the faith to outweigh what my human eyes can see. And when my time comes, I pray that I am ready to step up and show out. In Jesus Name. Amen!

All praises due to him who is the author and finisher of my life. Lord, I ask that you teach me Spiritual discipline. Encourage me to speak greatness and not failure. Remove negativity and replace it with positive affirmation. Thank You for making a way when I didn't or couldn't see it. Thank You in Advance for the blessings I am going to receive. In Jesus Name. Amen!

Father in heaven, today I release every care, concern, offense and disappointment to You. I will lean on You instead relying on my only faulty understanding of your ways. I choose to keep the peace that You have given me. I look forward to today knowing that You are with me and leading me in victory in Jesus' name! Amen.

I Thank You this morning for your touch which stirs my soul and excites my body to move. Lord, you are worthy of all the praise. I will bless your name at all times, you're praises shall continually be in my mouth. Thank You for my tests which ultimately become my testimony. For finding perfection in an perfectly flawed vessel, I am forever grateful. Bless me this day and every day as I go forward with direction and purpose. In Jesus Name. Amen!

I greet you this morning with all praise for allowing me to see another day. Thank You for filling my lungs with air, giving me activity of my mind and limbs and blessing me from head to toe. Let me not be led by emotion, but instead remind me to constantly speak and consult with you in all things. Direct my path so that I am in position when my blessings come. In Jesus Name. Amen!

Thank You Lord for placing your hand on my life. You gentle prodding and pruning at times seems uncomfortable, but in the end produces wonderful fruit. For keeping me safe in the face of imminent danger, I praise your name all the more. Bless me so that I may help to bless another. In Jesus Name. Amen!

As I rise this morning ready to conquer this new day and receive all the blessings within, I first kneel at the throne from which the most high reigns. Help me to not lean upon my own understanding, but in all things great and small acknowledge your hand on my life, listen for your voice and seek your face. Grant me your favor and blessings this day. In Jesus Name. Amen!

Thank You Lord for the blessings you wrapped up for me in the gift wrap called a new day. Thank You for the bow tied with grace and mercy. Thank You for giving me way more than I deserve and loving me way more than I could ever love myself. Lord as you are working in this season I ask that you don't do it without me. Bless me and my loved ones this evening, see us safely to the dawn of a new day. In Jesus Name. Amen!

As the seasons change and the time on the clock is set back, let us not forget to take/make the time to praise your name. Thank You Lord for never leaving or forsaking me when I did, said and thought those things that are far from holy. I ask that you continue to have patience with me while there is still much work to be done. Bless those that pray for me and those that plot against me. In Jesus Name. Amen!

My Father in heaven, the author and finisher of my life. Teach me to lean not unto my own, faulty often decided my emotion, understanding. Instead work in me and on me and increase my faith so that I trust you when I can't trace you, but I know you are always there. Help me to not focus on what my eyes can see but to follow my faith to heights only my mind can imagine. Craving your favor every day and every way. In Jesus Name. Amen!

My Father, My God! Thank you for extending me your favor to see this new day. Lord, I ask that you bless all within the width and breath of this digital communication. Meet us where we are and help us move upward and onward. Cover us with your blood from the crown of our heads to the souls of our feet. Protect us from the one whose sole purpose is to kill and destroy. In Jesus Name. Amen!

From the rising of the sun to the going down of the same, I will bless your name. Lord I Thank You for blessing me with yet another day on earth. Thank You for your word, your corrective guidance and your touch upon my life. I pray every day that I am prepared for the journey ahead. I pray that you will keep me mentally awake, physically able and spiritually strong. In Jesus Name. Amen

I rise this morning loudly proclaiming that You are my Lord and my God. I go forward with extremely high levels of enthusiasm prepared to meet this day and all of its challenges. I am reaching out and up to claim my blessings. Guide me through the darkness of the valley equip me with the tools necessary to see it through to the end. In Jesus Name. Amen!

Thank You Lord for walking with me this day. You kept me safe from dangers seen and unseen. Led me along the way and corrected me when I went astray. Gave me strength when I became weary and required nothing other than my obedience. You are an awesome God and worthy of all the praise. In Jesus Name. Amen!

Thank You Lord for the blessing of life this morning. I pray that you would find favor with your children this day. Protect us from those things that are crafted to harm us, protect us from ourselves. Let my mantra for today and always be "Thy will Not my will ". In the Mighty and matchless Name of Jesus! Amen.

Thank You Lord for this new day. I Thank You for keeping me safe from harm while I slumbered. I pray that I will take advantage of the gifts and talents that you have deposited within me. Thank You for blessing me so richly, allow me to be a blessing to another. I pray for those dealing with loss and grief this day. Surround them with your Love and uplift them. In Jesus Name! Amen.

Heavenly Father, Thank You for the life that you have given me to live. I Thank You for the forgiveness of sins and the daily renewal of Grace and Mercy. Teach us Lord to be Thankful for what we have as we know we could have less. Bless those less fortunate and keep us safe from hurt, harm or danger. In Jesus Name! Amen.

From the rising of the sun to the going down of the same, I continue to praise your Holy Name. I Thank You for your breath that fills my lungs and the activity of my mind and limbs. I pray this day that you would extend your hedge of protection to all who seek your face. In Jesus Name! Amen

Thank You Heavenly Father for your touch that wakes me this morning. I Thank You for your grace and mercy that sustains my being. Bless us Lord individually and collectively so that we may truly be about the business of saving souls and reaching others. Give us the strength to persevere this day. In Jesus Name! Amen

I rise this morning extremely grateful for another day. I Thank You for loving me in spite of me. I ask that You remove me and my agenda out of your way so that I may fully participate in the plan you have for my life. Use me so that I may be a light of hope for another. Hide me behind your hedge of protection so that I may escape harm, hurt or danger. In Jesus Name! Amen.

Thank You Lord for this day. I praise your name for allowing me to be counted amongst the living this day. Let my words and actions be acceptable in your sight this day. Thank You for the forgiveness of sins and the covering which is your Grace and Mercy. In Jesus Name! Amen.

Thank You Heavenly Father for the breath that fills my lungs this morning. Thank You for being my covering when the rain has fallen in my life. Thank You for being my biggest fan when all the odds seemed to be against me. You continue to do for me when I have been less than grateful and far from humble. Thank You for loving me in spite of me. This cracked and worn vessel stands in awe and worships you! Thanking You Always and in All Ways. In Jesus Name! Amen.

Thank You Lord for blessing me with this new day. I pray that I will be able to meet this day with the courage needed to overcome those obstacles that may come my way. When I feel defeated help me to remember that YOU have equipped me with all I need. Give me patience as I deal not only with others, but specifically with me. In Jesus Name! Amen

Thanking You Always and in All Ways for the bountiful blessings that you have allowed into my life. I praise your name for you have breathed life into my lungs, given me the activity of my mind and limbs and have filled me with your spirit. I Thank You for keeping me from harm, hurt or danger. Let me go forward this day with my eyes shut and my Faith wide open. In Jesus Name! Amen.

I humbly enter your presence one again to express how grateful I am that you have seen fit to allow me to see yet another day. I pray that you would heal the sick and uplift those who serve as their caretakers. I pray for those who are coming out of a storm as well as those who are entering the same. I ask that you would continue to bless your children and allow them to be blessings. In Jesus Name! Amen.

I lift my voice this morning praising your name for allowing me to wake this morning. I Thank You for safe passage through the storm last night, as well as those storms that occur in life. Father we ask that You would keep us safe from harm while teaching us to look toward you as we overcome the obstacles in life. Let each experience be one with an abundance of teaching and learning. Give us safe passage to and fro as we leave the peace and sanctity of our homes. Peace and blessings to all this day. In Jesus Name! Amen.

I rise this morning Thanking You Always and in All Ways for the Grace and Mercy which you have extended towards me. I am ever so grateful that you have allowed me yet another undeserved day. I pray for all that strive to be who you have created us to be. Let us not be detoured by what our eyes see, but excited for we know that with Faith all things are possible. Rain your blessings down upon us all. In Jesus Name! Amen

Thank You Lord for blessing me with a brand new day. I pray that those gifts and talents within me will manifest in due time so that I may live my life to its fullest potential. Keep me humble through the good days as well as the bad days. Teach me to count my blessings and to treat all obstacles as opportunities to draw closer to you. Bless all who acknowledge your presence. In Jesus Name! Amen.

Thank You Lord for your undeserved Grace and Mercy. I am Thankful to have you in my life. You continue to bless me even when I am bitter, or less than thankful for the blessings bestowed upon me. Draw me closer to you so that I may not be separated from you. Walking by faith and not by sight is my ultimate goal. Surround me with your hedge of protection. In Jesus Name! Amen

Thank You Lord for filling my lungs with your breath and for giving activity to my mind and limbs. Bless me Lord so that I may resist those temptations that would serve to separate me from you. Give me peace within as well as patience with others and myself. Keep me focused, faithful and humble. In Jesus Name! Amen.

All praise this morning to the One who is worthy of all the praise. We Thank You Lord for your goodness and mercy. We humbly enter your presence fully expecting to be blessed. I pray that you would heal the sick, comfort the weary and injured and uplift the downtrodden. Allow us, your children to be a blessing to others. Keep us safe from the evils that men do. In Jesus Name! Amen.

Thank You Lord for allowing me to see another day. Thank You for the renewal of Grace and Mercy. I pray for peace within and patience with myself. Fill me with your spirit so that I might walk right and talk right, forever bringing Glory and Honor to your name. In Jesus Name! Amen.

Thank You Lord for waking me this morning. I enter your presence with humility seeking your face this day. I pray that the words of my mouth and the meditations of my heart be acceptable in your sight this day. Keep me upright and steadfast in the work you have for me. In Jesus Name! Amen.

Thank You Lord for waking me this morning. I enter your presence with humility seeking your face this day. I pray that the words of my mouth and the meditations of my heart be acceptable in your sight this day. Keep me upright and steadfast in the work you have for me. In Jesus Name! Amen.

Thank You Lord for this new day, full of blessings and new opportunities. I Thank You for the sun that shines above as well as the son that radiates from within. I pray for blessings for the sinner as well as the saint. Make keen my steps so that I may avoid obstacles and pitfalls that might knock me off of my true path. In Jesus Name! Amen.

Thank You Lord for your touch that woke me from my slumber. Thank You for the warm blood that flows through my veins and for allowing me full control of my limbs and mind. I pray that I might be able to bless another to some degree as you have so richly blessed me. Let me not be arrogant in my dealings with others, but with humility and dignity show the world whose I am. In Jesus Name! Amen.

I rise Thanking You for yet another day. I pray for all who might need someone to stand in the gap for them today. I pray for men, women, husbands, wives, single parents and most of all our children. Father when I feel lost and confused, I ask that you clear my mind and direct my path. Remind me that I walk by Faith and NOT by sight. Surround your children with your hedge of protection not allowing harm, hurt or danger to affect our lives. In Jesus Name! Amen.

Thank You Lord for this brand new day. Thank You for the renewal of Grace and Mercy daily, not because I am so righteous, but because You are so good to me. Thank You for delivering me from my sins. Teach me to lean on those teachings that have prepared me for the shifts in life. I pray for peace and blessings for all who would recognize you as Lord and Savior. In Jesus Name! Amen.

Thank You for blessing me with this new day. Bless me so that I may be a blessing. Keep my mind focused on You. Direct my thoughts, actions and words so that I may represent your hand on my life. Forgive me of my sins and keep me humble through this journey called life. Let me remain teachable through both my triumphs and my failures. In Jesus Name! Amen.

Heavenly Father I rise this morning praising your name for allowing me to see another day. I Thank You for your grace and mercy that sustains me. I pray that your blessings would follow me far and wide and allow me to uplift another. Surround my friends and family with your hedge of protection. In Jesus Name! Amen.

Thank You Lord for blessing me to see another day. Forgive me of my sins both of commission and omission. Open my eyes to see the manifestation of your Grace and Mercy. Open my ears so that I may hear your voice void of distraction. Open my heart to receive all that you have to pour into me. Walking by faith and not by sight is my ultimate goal. In Jesus Name! Amen.

Most gracious and merciful Heavenly Father I come humbly before you this morning Thanking You for undeserved blessings. I pray for healing, physically, mentally and spiritually. Allow my experiences to teach me to be Thankful, not taking anything for granted. Give me the patience necessary to face difficulties with grace and honor to your name and credit for whose I am. In Jesus Name! Amen.

Thank You Lord for blessing me with this new day. Open my eyes so that I may better appreciate all that you have done for me. Surround me with your hedge of protection so that I may escape those things which may cause me harm. In Jesus Name! Amen.

Made in the USA
Coppell, TX
30 January 2023